The Revolutionary War

War

By John M. Thompson

VOLUNTEERS
WANTED

WAR
LIBERTY
RIGHTS

NATIONAL GEOGRAPHIC

WASHINGTON, D. C.

Battles
of the
American Revolution
1775-1783

NORTH AMERICA

Lake Michigan

Lake Huron

Lake Ontario

Lake Erie

Mississippi

Quebec 🇬🇧

Montreal

MASS.
(DISTRICT
OF MAINE)

St. Lawrence

FT. TICONDEROGA
Oriskany Saratoga
Bennington

N.H.

Lexington
Albany MASS. Bunker Hill
NEW YORK Concord Boston
CONN. R.I.

FT. DETROIT

BRITISH

WEST POINT
White Plains
Wyoming New York November 1776
Massacre FT. LEE AND FT. WASHINGTON
PA. Morristown Long Island
FORT Princeton Monmouth Courthouse
AUGUSTA Germantown
VALLEY FORGE Trenton
Brandywine Philadelphia
N.J.
DEL.

FT. PITT

FT. HENRY

Cahokia

Vincennes

Kaskaskia

Ohio

Tennessee

MARYLAND

Potomac

Chesapeake Bay

VIRGINIA

James

Richmond
Williamsburg

Yorktown

APPALACHIAN

Guilford
Courthouse

NORTH CAROLINA

Cowpens

King's
Mountain

Charlotte

FT. NINETY SIX Camden

Augusta

SOUTH
CAROLINA

Wilmington

GEORGIA

Savannah

Charleston

Alabama

Savannah

SPANISH LOUISIANA

ATLANTIC OCEAN

EAST FLORIDA
(Under British control
from   -   )

Gulf of Mexico

British North America, 1775 (excluding 13 colonies)
The 13 Colonies
Spanish possessions
American victory
British victory
Indecisive battle
■ Fort

0   miles   200
0   kilometers   300

From Savannah to Quebec, from the Atlantic to the Mississippi, battles for freedom raged, opposite.
PRECEDING PAGES: *In 1775, ardent colonists raised the liberty pole, signal and symbol, in many a town square.*

With colonists distrustful of British authority, the city of Boston was a powder keg ready to explode.

*Ships of trade glided in and out of Boston Harbor constantly during the 1760s and early
1770s, bringing European goods to the colonies and carrying American raw materials
back to the mother country. Irked by tariffs on commerce, political leaders such as
Samuel Adams and John Hancock helped make Boston a flashpoint of the Revolution.*

Chapter One

It was raining in Boston on Tuesday, May 17, 1774. Water was puddling in the streets and a stiff east wind was blowing. But the foul weather was not enough to stop a crowd of thousands from gathering down at the wharf to gape at a certain British ship of war. Drums began a low tattoo, followed by a deafening salutation of guns and the pealing of church bells. Down the ship's gangplank strode an impressive parade of officials in dazzling red jackets and white breeches trimmed with gold. And then the main attraction himself: the Honorable Thomas Gage, newly appointed Governor of the Province of Massachusetts Bay and Commander in Chief of His Majesty's forces in America.

The crowd followed the procession of horses, grenadiers, artillerymen, and militia to the State House, where the governor was officially presented by proclamation. Three volleys of musket fire and appropriate huzzas from the assembled masses welcomed him to Massachusetts.

Everything went off without a hitch, down to the formal toasts at the Faneuil Hall reception. The whole arrival was a properly executed display of fanfare and decorum—but the colonists gathered to witness the event knew better. Their huzzas were automatic, hollow, and no doubt in many cases sardonic. If there was excitement in the air, it was over something else, something new that they could almost feel. The winds of change were blowing—not for a new governor but for a whole new kind of government.

They eyed the man appointed by their mother country of Great Britain to rule them. Good-looking, dignified, even-tempered, and respected, Gage had served in America before. He was returning to replace another governor, who had made himself unpopular by urging Parliament to repress the rebellious colonists. Gage's mission was anything but friendly—in fact, it was almost bound to stir smoldering resentment into flames. Authorized to put as many soldiers in the city as he deemed

PRECEDING PAGES: *The "Boston Massacre" of March 5, 1770, was started by a mob heckling British soldiers. The death of five citizens galvanized anti-British sentiment.*

In 1775, Boston was nearly
an island; the Back Bay
was filled in by the late
19th century. To the north,
Bunker Hill offered higher
ground and a military
advantage: It was the site of
the war's first battle.

PLAN OF THE TOWN OF BOSTON WITH THE
ATTACK on BUNKER'S-HILL in the Peninsula of CHARLESTOWN,
the 17th of June 1775.

necessary to maintain order; Gage had also been given power to pardon anyone who went beyond the call of duty for Britain's sake. He was charged with closing the port of Boston, and that action could throttle the city's industry and bring its citizens to their knees—which was, after all, his main objective. Lately His Majesty's subjects in Boston had not done much genuflecting. In fact, they had sacked the previous governor's mansion, had dumped shipments of British tea into the harbor, and now openly flouted authority. Gage was in Massachusetts to crack down.

Gen. Thomas Gage, appointed governor of Massachusetts in 1774, directed British troops in what became the first battles of the Revolution. The once popular leader faced an increasingly volatile situation. After the Battle of Bunker Hill in 1775, Parliament replaced him.

HOW HAD BOSTON TURNED INTO an us-versus-them powder keg, with a citizenry so distrustful of authority it was ready to explode? In 1763 Americans were generally happy under loose British rule—or, as one prime minister called it, "salutary neglect." Yes, there were trade restrictions and import duties on molasses, but enforcement was lax. Smuggling was winked at, especially if smoothed over by a case of good port wine. After all, the trade system was set up to make Britain competitive with other countries, and America, as part of the empire, was a beneficiary.

At the end of the costly Seven Years' War (called the French and Indian War in America), Britain sank into deep debt and set her sights on her prosperous American colonies. The Sugar Act of 1764, raising the duty on sugar, was the first of many measures to cause anger, not for any hardship it imposed but for its stated purpose: It was nothing less than a means of collecting revenue from the pockets of the colonists.

But the measure that really raised hackles along the eastern seaboard was the infamous Stamp Act of 1765. According to this new law, most legal and business documents and many everyday items—newspapers, pamphlets, playing cards, for example—had to be made of paper bearing an embossed impression. The cost of the stamped paper was modest, but penalties could be assessed for noncompliance. Similar stamps were routinely used in Great Britain, but the American colonists, who had never had to pay for stamps before, cried foul at what they saw as an unprecedented attempt by Parliament to tax them directly. Those hit hardest by the Stamp Act—writers, printers, lawyers, and gamblers—were those England could least afford to antagonize.

A Stamp Act Congress convened in New York in October 1765 to coordinate resistance. The Congress declared that, with all due respect to the crown, since the colonists were not represented in Parliament, it had no right to tax them. In truth, few colonists wanted to be represented in Parliament. They knew that American votes would be swamped by British votes, since Britain had a much larger population. And England

FOLLOWING PAGES: Where pigs and chickens once walked dirt lanes, 180-year-old Quincy Market and the adjacent 260-year-old Faneuil Hall still thrive with food vendors on Boston's Freedom Trail.

The Revolutionary War

had become, in the eyes of many Americans, a sinkhole of political corruption, dominated by special interests—no place for the virtuous American colonists, even if they were offered seats in Parliament.

Resistance to the Stamp Act sometimes grew violent. Citizens in Boston hanged the stamp officer in effigy and hounded him out of office, then vandalized the governor's mansion. In ports up and down the coast, stamps were destroyed, and stamp officers resigned in fear. On the day the act went into effect, flags flew at half-staff and church bells tolled in mourning. A few stamps sold in the sparsely settled colony of Georgia, but to the north, not one colonial governor tried to enforce the law. Buyers and sellers simply ignored it, and business went on as before, documents circulating without stamps.

Some members of Parliament insisted that force should be used to put the unruly Americans in their place. For the time being, however, wiser heads prevailed. William Pitt, the influential First Earl of Chatham and a tireless champion of American rights, eloquently argued the unconstitutionality of taxation without representation, adding, "I rejoice that America has resisted." The law was repealed, followed by an outburst of gratitude and merrymaking in the colonies, where people shot off fireworks, drank toasts to the King, and commissioned portraits of Pitt and other supporters of the American cause.

Now, however, an interesting legal and diplomatic dilemma arose. If the colonists got their way this time, what was to keep them from doing it again, and again? Afflicted with gout and other infirmities, William Pitt left public life. His post was taken up by an outspoken young man named Charles Townshend, Chancellor of the Exchequer, known to the British as "Champagne Charley" for the speech he once gave while drunk. Townshend had no patience with or understanding of colonial America. He came up with a

Before colonists backed up slogans with actions, they began waging a revolution of the mind. Even household items like this teapot could become political statements. Paul Revere's engraving of the Boston Massacre, opposite, was sheer propaganda, inaccurately showing redcoats firing on command.

scheme to placate the Americans. Relying on the premise that the colonies did not object to "external taxes" (duties on imports) as they did to "internal taxes" (domestic duties, such as the Stamp Act), he put forth bills establishing taxes on British glass, paper, paint, and tea arriving in colonial ports and legalizing searches to enforce taxation. The income from the new taxes would pay the salaries of colonial governors and judges.

Colonists started boycotting English goods. Resistance groups formed. In Boston, an angry mob attacked officials who had seized *Liberty,* a sloop owned by John Hancock. One of Boston's richest merchants, Hancock was a resistance leader, a suspected smuggler, and a nuisance to the British. When two regiments arrived in Boston, sent to quell the unrest, citizens refused to house them. Benjamin Franklin, in London as a lobbyist for several colonies, astutely observed, "You are putting young soldiers, who are by nature insolent, in the midst of a people who consider themselves threatened and oppressed. It's like setting up a blacksmith's forge in a magazine of gunpowder."

That magazine would blow in early March 1770. For a couple of years, the tension between the soldiers and townspeople of Boston had been growing, each side egging the other on to greater acts of violence. Name-calling had turned to brawls on more than one occasion. A fight in early March involving soldiers and workmen had been broken up before it had concluded to everyone's satisfaction. Both sides agreed they needed to resume the conflict. On the fifth of March, there was an electric buzz in the air. The fight not picking up where it left off, a restive mob began roaming the streets looking for action. About 50 people gathered around a sentinel in front of the customs house. The sentinel called out for help, and a captain summoned seven men from the British main guard. Instead of leaving, the mob grew even more bellicose, taking on a personality of its own. They had come out for a fight, and they were going to get one. They began swearing at the troops, then throwing snowballs and rocks. Fists and clubs began flying. A soldier hit the ground. Someone yelled "Fire!" When the smoke from the muskets had cleared, five civilians lay dead, with six more wounded.

The news shot like lightning through the city. Thomas Hutchinson, the British-sent lieutenant governor of Massachusetts, went out among the crowd. By promising to bring the responsible soldiers to trial, he talked everyone into going home and, not long afterward, requested that the troops leave the city to restore the peace. Two prominent locals agitated for an immediate trial: Samuel Adams, a failed brewer turned firebrand propagandist, now on a meteoric rise to the top of Britain's most-wanted list, and John Hancock, the businessman who was a member of the legislature and would become the first governor of Massachusetts.

But the trial was put off until autumn, so that tempers could cool and the accused would receive fair play. Ultimately only two soldiers were convicted of manslaughter, the others acquitted on pleas of self-defense. One of the lawyers defending the soldiers was John Adams, a distant cousin of Samuel, who decried Parliament's claims over the colonies but wanted to prove that Americans were principled, law-abiding people.

Propaganda machines run by Samuel Adams and others did not wait around for the outcome of the trial. The whole affair was reported by the American press as the "Boston Massacre," the slain honored as martyrs. Years later, on the anniversary date, a Whig orator recalled it, asking, "Has the grim savage rushed again from the wilderness? Or does some fiend, fierce from the depths of hell . . . twang her deadly arrows at our breast? No, none of these—it is the hand of Britain that inflicts the wound."

Meanwhile, Parliament was already considering a repeal of the Townshend duties. The resulting compromise had a curious way of further infuriating hot tempers. Intending to reserve the sovereign right to tax subjects

George III

Who was this man whom Americans saw as their enemy? Thomas Paine dubbed King George III the "Royal Brute." In fact, he was not a ruthless tyrant, nor a brilliant strategist, nor a fool. He assumed the throne in 1760 at the age of 22. He ruled in the wake of a bitter civil war, which had ended by vesting sovereign power in Parliament. Moderately talented, he wanted to be known as a benevolent monarch. He respected the governing body's authority but manipulated it to gain his own ends, frequently changing ministers to assure that Parliamentary decrees followed traditional Tory paths.

During the American Revolution, the relationship between George III and his ministers was poorly understood, especially in America. Not until Thomas Paine published *Common Sense* did the target of American opposition to Britain's repressive policies encompass not only Parliament but also the King himself. It finally dawned on the colonists that their King was not simply being misguided, but that in fact he was the one who was wielding the punishing rod.

Five years into George III's reign, he had suffered a brief bout of mental illness. The illness returned in 1788, long after the American Revolution was over. Given the King's increasingly muddled mind, his eldest son served as Prince Regent from 1811 until his death in 1820. That son took the throne as George IV, one of Great Britain's least distinguished monarchs.

In December 1773, defiant Sons of Liberty dressed as Mohawks and, cheered on by spectators, paddled into moonlit Boston Harbor and deep-sixed 342 chests of East India House tea. By destroying the 10,000-pound cargo, participants in the Boston Tea Party took a dramatic stand against taxes on goods sold to the colonies by the British.

in the colonies, Parliament designated just one item of trade as still taxable: tea. "I am clear that there must always be one tax to keep up the right," said King George, "and as such I approve of the tea duty."

In May 1770, a London newspaper lambasted Parliament, declaring that "in the repeal of those acts, which were most offensive to America, they have done every thing but remove the offence." Edmund Burke, the brilliant Whig orator, questioned British actions, and about one-third of the House of Commons sided with him throughout the war. Prophetically, in April 1774 Burke implored the government not to tax the colonies just to prove its right to do so. Let America tax herself, he argued,

The Revolutionary War

and "be content to bind America by laws of trade." Despite Burke's eloquence, the tea tax remained.

THE COLONIES SETTLED BACK DOWN for two more years of relative peace and quiet, but that tax remained a thorn in the side. Americans dropped their general boycott of British goods but still refused to buy British tea. Instead of letting the issue die out, thus taking the wind from the sails of American agitators, Britain imprudently decided to meddle. Frederick, Lord North came up with a surefire scheme for making Americans buy British tea and thus pay the British tax.

The man who would be prime minister for nearly the entire American Revolution, Lord North was well liked in Parliament—fat, tall, pop-eyed, and large-nosed, he was honest and good-humored. He would applaud a particularly fine speech, even one made against him. Like many in Parliament, though, he knew little about the colonies 3,000 miles away. He was not anti-American like Townshend, but he *was* a Tory, believing in Parliament's supremacy and supporting King George.

North's scheme must have looked brilliant to his Tory countrymen. In early 1773 the East India Company, Britain's premier tea trader—a corporation chartered by the crown, which ruled India with its own private army—was almost bankrupt. Once Americans decided to boycott British tea, immense quantities of tea began piling up, rotting in company warehouses. The East India Company's wealthy stock-holders—many of them members of Parliament—were furious. So North proposed that Parliament allow the company to sell tea stripped of all duties except the Townshend tax. Americans would get cheaper tea, and the East India Company could unload its warehouses.

North underestimated the Americans. To them it looked like bribery, an underhanded way of forcing them to accept an unconstitutional tax. Compounding his blunder, North allowed the arrangement for only select American merchants. Those not chosen, including John Hancock, were outraged. Creative minds immediately set to work trying to figure how to keep the insidious tea from the public. The answer? They would not allow it to be unloaded, and if it was, they would confiscate it. A series of tea parties were organized up and down the coast. Boston's was the first and most dramatic, giving the name "tea party" to these acts of civil disobedience. In New York, Philadelphia, Annapolis, and Charleston,

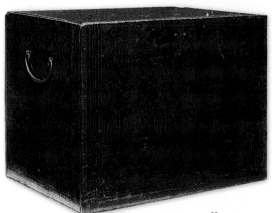

resistors prevented tea-laden ships from landing.

In Boston on December 16, 1773, a band of local men disguised as Mohawk Indians boarded three East India ships at anchor. A large crowd gathered to watch, silent but approving. By the end, the raiders had tossed 342 chests of tea into Boston Harbor—worth as much as $150,000 in today's economy. Britain answered with a series of repressive laws, known in America as the Intolerable Acts and in Britain as the Coercive Acts. The most offensive—and the most counterproductive—of them all was the Boston Port Act, which ordered the port blockaded and closed to

commerce. Unemployed longshoremen, sailors, and warehouse workers now roamed about freely, looking for targets on which to vent their anger. Coupled with a forced reduction of local self-government, the action was almost certain to generate backlash. What King George, Lord North, and other Britons could not grasp was that the harder they clamped down, the more firmly the colonists resisted. Meanwhile, a new generation in America was beginning to pit the rights of man—in modern parlance, their human rights—against their constitutional rights as Englishmen.

INTO THIS UNTENABLE SITUATION strode Gage, Massachusetts' new governor, on May 17, 1774. When he found that the colony's legislature would not pay for the spilt tea, he declared it dissolved and ordered more troops sent to the city. As support for British policy eroded around him, Gage dug himself in deeper, not seeing that the rising tide would at some point inevitably break over him. On September 1, 1774, afraid that a Yankee militia would take 125 barrels of gunpowder from a storehouse in Cambridge, Gage sent 250 British redcoats to seize it. The move was seen by locals as hostile and invasive.

Four days later, at the urging of Massachusetts, representatives from 12 of the 13 colonies met to form the First Continental Congress in

Boston was a blur of activity in May 1774 as British troops arrived. Up to that time, Britain had maintained power in its American colonies by trade controls over items such as tea. The elegant Chinese lacquer tea chest, opposite, washed ashore in Boston Harbor the day after the infamous Tea Party of December 16, 1773.

Tyranny, like hell, is not easily conquered . . .
the harder the conflict,
the more glorious the triumph.

THOMAS PAINE, *The Crisis, Number 1*, 1776

Philadelphia. Delegates to this convention were elected illegally by colonial legislatures, unauthorized to do so by the colonial governors. Their plan was to meet privately, outside the government structure sanctioned by the ruling British, to consider ways to safeguard American liberties. There was no talk yet of independence, merely of redress for their grievances as free British subjects. For the first time the colonies, which up to now had thought of themselves as separate entities under the British crown, began coming together for a common cause. As they united with a single voice, they foreshadowed a new nation.

Citizens began to see themselves as more American than British. And they resented the superior attitude of their European cousins. This was expressed in the extreme by Lord Sandwich, First Lord of the Admiralty, who considered Americans "the most treacherous, infamous, worthless race of men that God ever permitted to inhabit the earth." One can only wonder why he fought to keep them British.

Parliament's answer to the Continental Congress was to call for more coercion and more repression. For the next several months, the patriots (as they had begun calling themselves) and the British began preparations for war. In London, the monarch seemed content. "I am not sorry," wrote George III, "that the line of conduct seems now chalked out. . . . The New England Governments are in a state of rebellion. Blows must decide whether they are to be subject to the Country [Great Britain] or Independent." Determining that force was the only way to put the unruly Americans in their place, the British dispatched more troops to Boston. Gage was instructed to move quickly against the rebels.

As 1774 drew to a close, armed conflict appeared more and more likely. Many in America paused for breath. The choice was to accept moderate oppression or reach for uncertain freedom, even possible chaos. Gradually political lines were drawn between loyalists (or Tories, as they were called) and patriots. Many colonists rejected Parliament's attempt to curtail their liberties, but the disagreement came over what to do about it. Organizations like the Sons of Liberty practiced their own kind of tyranny by boycotting British goods. Formed to oppose the Stamp Act, the Sons of Liberty clogged the wheels of British government through propaganda, assemblies, petitions, and outright violence. Many who disagreed with them were fingered, censured, even tarred and feathered. Caught up in the clamor for change, families often were divided in their sympathies, and a multitude of small tragedies unfolded across the land in America's first civil war.

By majorities of two to one, both the House of Lords and the House of Commons determined in early 1775 that the colonies should bow to Britain. Massachusetts was declared to be in a state of rebellion. Parliament sent more troops to America. New England's maritime trade was limited by parliamentary decree to Britain and the British West Indies. In a series of famous speeches seeking conciliation with America, Edmund Burke tried once again to appeal to his fellow parliamentarians, cautioning wisely on March 22, 1775, "The use of force alone is but *temporary*. It may subdue for a moment; but it does not remove the necessity of subduing again: and a nation is not governed, which is perpetually to be conquered."

The speeches of the Whigs were all in vain. The die was cast, and neither side was backing down. Less than a month after Burke's words, the American Revolution began.

Revolutionary spirits laid to rest in Boston's Old Granary Burying Ground include patriot leaders Paul Revere, John Hancock, John and Samuel Adams, as well as those slain in the 1773 Boston Massacre. Dating from 1660, the graveyard was named for a grain storage building on the site.

How the Age of Enlightenment

The ideas of 18th-century philosophers Voltaire and Rousseau, above, changed people's ideas and expectations as dramatically as did James Watt's steam engine, opposite, one of the key inventions during the age of the American Revolution.

What was the intellectual backdrop against which the American Revolution played? From the mid-1700s to the mid-1800s, first Great Britain, then the rest of Europe experienced the sweeping Industrial Revolution. A gradual shift from an agricultural to an industrial way of life was occurring, culminating in the establishment of large factories and the mass production of textiles, all of which was made possible by machines such as James Watt's steam engine, patented in 1769, and James Hargreaves's spinning jenny, patented in 1770.

Meanwhile, 18th-century philosophers were expounding the tenets of the Enlightenment. They believed in handling social and religious problems rationally and scientifically, and thus held a more secular world view. To Enlightenment philosophers, spiritual authority and dogmatism were often roadblocks to change, which was considered good, a move toward improvement. The very idea of progress was an Enlightenment invention. The French author and philosopher Voltaire, one of the most influential thinkers of his time, inveighed against injustice and intolerance. His witty, unorthodox views, such as those expressed in the satirical novel *Candide,* had a profound effect on the political leaders of the age. His countryman Jean-Jacques Rousseau argued in *The Social Contract,* published in 1762, that no one has any natural authority over anyone else, and therefore each citizen has equal obligations to all.

Earlier, 17th-century English philosopher John Locke had written that a government is a trust, meant to protect the inherent rights of the people, namely the right to life, liberty, and property. Furthermore, argued Locke, if a government abused these rights, the people had the right to rebel and create a new government. His ideas had so worked their way into the fabric of monarchical Britain that by the time of the

Inspired a Revolution

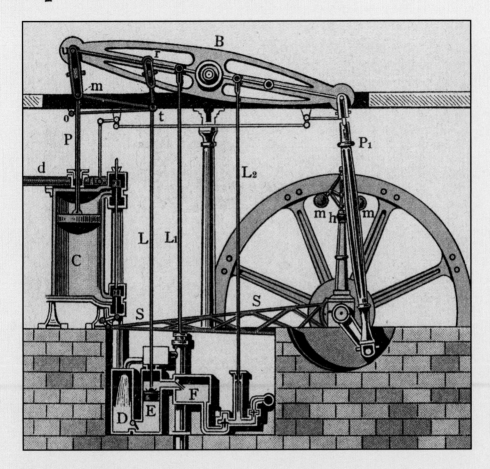

American Revolution, George III could accurately state that "no people ever enjoyed more happiness or lived under a milder Government than those now revolted Provinces." The problem was that the colonists envisioned an even better form of government than the one ruling from afar—one that had not yet been invented. The leaders whose spirit infused the American Revolution, and the French Revolution soon after, owed much to the ideas of Locke, Rousseau, Voltaire, and other Enlightenment thinkers.

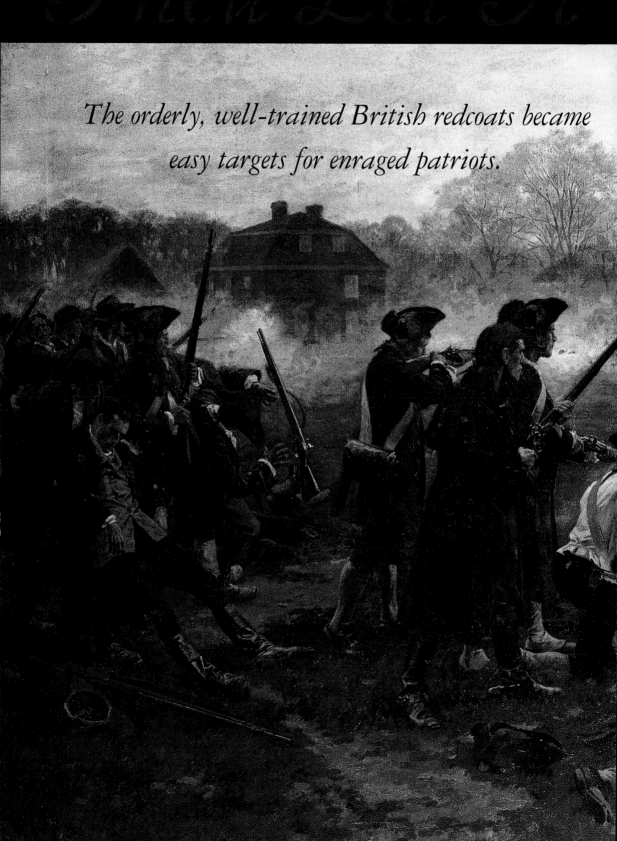

The orderly, well-trained British redcoats became easy targets for enraged patriots.

Minding the music and the step, fifers and drummers enspirited soldiers throughout the war. Music measured out the daily rhythms of life—reveille, strike the tent, march, halt, attack, and parley. Often the music was just for fun. A sprightly tune once played by the British to insult Americans became the most popular among American fifers: "Yankee Doodle."

Chapter Two

In the early months of 1775, General Gage built up his forces until about 4,000 soldiers had crossed the Atlantic to join him in the American colonies. He sent repeated requests back to his homeland, asking for an army 20,000 strong, but they were repeatedly denied by the British cabinet. Frustrated, he sent what troops he had on training marches into the countryside, readying them for action.

The voters of Massachusetts ignored Gage's authority and the British law he had been sent there to wield. They elected their own delegates and established an illegal and self-constituted body called the Provincial Congress of Massachusetts.

The Provincial Congress first met in Cambridge in February 1775, and in Concord, about 20 miles to the northwest, soon after. As their president the congress appointed 38-year-old John Hancock, the wealthy merchant from Braintree who was at that time already a member of the Massachusetts General Court. He urged citizens to defend themselves against the encroachments of the British Army. Local militia units were appointed as the vanguard of defense should Gage's troops take any hostile action. Intending to be ready at a minute's notice, they took the name "minutemen" and gathered a cache of military supplies at Concord.

Gage's spies reported back on these developments. Gage now had to act, or the rebels would be able to seize the advantage. On the night of April 18, 1775, he sent a detachment of 700 troops to destroy the supplies at Concord. Ferried across Boston Harbor, the soldiers began marching to Lexington as quietly as possible.

Like so many episodes of the Revolution, the march to Lexington was no secret. No matter how hard generals tried to keep their intentions veiled, the network of spies on both sides was constantly busy, carrying and intercepting valuable information. Before the redcoats

PRECEDING PAGES: On April 19, 1775, war dawned on Lexington as eight minutemen died in an unexpected volley from British light infantry.

On April 18-19, 1775, Paul Revere traversed the countryside, warning of the British approach. A patrol captured him and threatened, "If you go an inch further, you are a dead man!"

had set foot on the mainland, patriot couriers were riding hard out of Boston, spreading word of the enemy's approach.

Three men carried the news. Forty-year-old Paul Revere, a master silversmith, was the main rider appointed by Boston's Committee of Safety. He rowed across the river to Charlestown, borrowed a horse, and set off toward Lexington, assigned to alert Samuel Adams and John Hancock, known to be there, that the British were after them. William Dawes, a second rider, rode down the narrow Boston Neck, through Cambridge, and west to Lexington, where he joined Revere. They delivered their message then continued on to Concord, joined by a third rider, Dr. Samuel Prescott. All three were arrested by the British. Dawes and Prescott escaped; Revere was quickly released. The entire episode took four hours, from 10 p.m. to 2 a.m. By the time Paul Revere returned to Lexington, a battle had begun.

Alerted by lights, drums, and church bells, a motley group of some 70 militiamen had assembled on the village green, preparing to face off with the approaching redcoats. At 4:30 a.m., more than an hour before sunrise, Maj. John Pitcairn, commanding officer of the British advance guard, rode into town leading almost 400 heavily armed men. "Lay down your arms, you damned rebels, and disperse!" he shouted.

"Stand your ground," ordered John Parker, the captain of the American militia. "Don't fire unless fired upon; but if they mean to have a war, let it begin here!" His men were beginning to move off, still carrying their muskets, when a shot rang out. No one knows who fired it and whether it was on purpose, but it triggered a volley from the redcoats, which was returned by a few of the fleeing militia. The redcoats then charged with bayonets. Pitcairn tried to keep his men back and later denied that he had ordered them to fire.

Within two minutes, the melee was over. Eight Americans were killed, including Parker, with ten wounded. One British soldier was grazed in the leg. The Revolutionary War had begun.

The Revolutionary War

But the day's events had not ended. Pitcairn's men gave a wild cheer, pleased that finally they were able to strike after months and even years of harassment. Little did they realize what they had touched off. Joined by grenadiers, who had formed the detachment's rear guard, the entire British force marched a few miles on to Concord, where they found that most of the military stores had already been moved by the rebels.

At the North Bridge over the Concord River, several hundred militiamen from surrounding towns came out against the redcoats. Now that blood had been spilled, there was little hesitation on either side, and after a short but heated conflict at the bridge, the redcoats converged back on the town. By noon, with nothing more to accomplish, the British decided to return to Boston. What they did not know was that the bloodiest part of the day was yet to come.

As the orderly, well-trained British soldiers marched back along the only road to Boston, they became easy targets for the enraged patriots. From stone walls and orchards, from barns and houses, the guns of the militia blazed away, picking off the highly visible redcoats. Soldiers by the dozen fell dead in the road. The British returned fire and burned

A reenactment echoes the chaos at Lexington on April 19, 1775. British soldiers faced off against 70 volunteers, only 8 of whom died. Lexington was the first battle of many in the American Revolution.

several buildings, but their main goal was to hustle back to safety. If not for a rescue column with two artillery pieces to clear the way, the slaughter would have been wholesale. Not able to reach the city directly, the British had to cut left and march down Charlestown Neck to Bunker Hill and the protection of the navy. By nightfall, the engagement's final tally was 73 British dead, with 174 wounded and 26 missing; and 49 Americans dead, 41 wounded, and 5 missing.

Many leaders in England had thought it unlikely that the Americans would actually fight back. Lexington and Concord proved them wrong. Not only had they fought: They fought well. If they had operated under a more unified command, in fact, they might have crushed the British. April 19, 1775, was in many ways a microcosm of the great struggle to come. The Americans would take a beating; then the British would pursue them deeper into the interior and hence farther from their supply bases. The deeper in the British went, the more militia swarmed around them, forcing them back.

The battle news spread so quickly through New England that by the morning of April 20, a ragtag army of 15,000 patriots had assembled around Boston, hemming the British in. Instead of negotiating an armistice with the colonials, Gage insisted that hostilities would cease when the patriots turned over their weapons. Attempts at a quick resolution evaporated in the next few weeks. After this initial battle, neither side was in the mood to negotiate; instead they began preparing for more widespread war.

As war broke out in America, Great Britain was the world's dominant colonial empire. Her 11 million people equalled only about half the population of France, but thanks largely to a huge and profitable trade network, England was Europe's superpower. Among Britain's holdings in India, the Caribbean, and elsewhere, none was as valuable as the colonies in North America. Their population in 1775 stood at two and a half million. That this figure had increased by a factor of ten over the past 75 years gave Britain pause. The mother country had never expected that her American child would grow so rapidly—it had just happened. And there was every indication that the child would keep growing at the same rate, doubling in population every 16 years.

Britain faced a daunting task in subduing her colonies. Time and again, the British counted on loyalist support in America, and time and again they were disappointed. The terrain in America was more

The Midnight Ride of Dawes, Prescott, and Revere
April 18–19, 1775

North Bridge
South Bridge
Concord
British retreat begins.
Prescott
Revere captured; Dawes escapes on foot. The ride is continued by Samuel Prescott.
Samuel Prescott joins Dawes and Revere outside of Lexington.
Lexington
Medford
Arlington
Mystic
Bunker Hill
Breed's Hill
Charlestown
Cambridge
Old North Church
Boston
Boston Harbor
Charles
Brookline
Roxbury
Sudbury

Paul Revere's route
William Dawes's route (continued by Samuel Prescott)
American militia
British column

N

miles 0 — 8
kilometers 0 — 12

rugged than the European battlefields known to the British. More than a thousand miles, connected by poor roads, separated the villages of New England and the rice plantations of Georgia.

What's worse, there was no capital—no one strategic and symbolic city—to be conquered. With its 40,000 people, Philadelphia was the biggest city in the colonies; indeed, it was one of the biggest in the British Empire. New York had a population of 25,000; Boston, 16,000; Charleston and Newport, over 10,000 each. Even when Philadelphia was the meeting place for the Continental Congress, it was not that meaningful a prize to capture: Congress could (and did) simply move elsewhere. Another difficulty the British military faced was that supplies, messages, and troops had to sail across the Atlantic: a six-week journey— in favorable weather. On the other hand, the British military did have the advantage of a sense of unity, which had not developed among the colonists. So far, any tactics waged against the redcoats had been planned on the spot, locally, by volunteer militia.

ON MAY 10, 1775, the Second Continental Congress convened in Philadelphia. The meeting had been arranged back in September by the First Congress, no one knowing that a state of war would exist by May. There was now pressing business, since fighting had broken out in Massachusetts. Again, all the colonies were represented except Georgia: In that small and distant colony, which still needed British arms to defend against an Indian uprising, the royal governor prevented the election of delegates and the passing of resolutions calling for economic sanctions. By the end of the year 1775, though, Georgia would join the others in a unified effort against the British.

Listen, my children, and you shall hear of the midnight ride of Paul Revere, William Dawes, and Samuel Prescott. Revere left Boston by water, Dawes by land. Then they met and carried the word of approaching British troops to patriots farther inland.

The list of those attending the Second Continental Congress is impressive. Representing Virginia were George Washington—43 years old, a soldier, surveyor, landowner, and member of the House of Burgesses—and Patrick Henry, 40, a prominent lawyer who seven weeks earlier had stirred the Virginia Convention by declaring, "Is life so dear, or peace so sweet, as to be purchased at the price of chains and slavery? Forbid it, Almighty God! I know not what course others may take, but as for me, give me liberty or give me death!" Samuel and John Adams, 54 and 41 years old, distant cousins to one another, represented Massachusetts. From New York came 31-year-old John Jay, who would become a chief justice of the U.S. Supreme Court, and from Pennsylvania, 41-year-old lawyer and essayist John Dickinson. Two important delegates, new to the Second Congress, were Pennsylvanian Benjamin Franklin, at 70 years old already known around the world as a scientist and pseudo-rustic philosopher, and Virginian Thomas Jefferson, a 33-year-old lawyer, landowner, and member of the House of Burgesses.

John Adams suggested that the troops congregating around Boston be forged into a Continental Army, so the American effort would be concentrated, not a diffuse confederation of regional militia. The key question was who would be the Army's commander. John Hancock wanted to be considered, but he had never seen military action. Moreover, he was from New England, the hotbed of rebellion. Most members of Congress agreed that a leader from outside that region would bring more unity to the struggle. Clearly, Southerners and Yankees were already somewhat suspicious of each other.

As the delegates looked around the room, they recognized that the most qualified man was there among them. Though he had never won any major victories, George Washington had served in two campaigns of the French and Indian War and had proven himself a brave and capable leader. He knew the lay of the land—as a young man, he had surveyed much of it. A wealthy planter, Washington was tall, strong, and dignified in carriage. He looked every inch the commander in chief. But what made him so effective, and thus Congress's choice of him so crucial, was his substance. The only real alternatives were British-born former officers of the British Army, like Charles Lee and Horatio Gates, who had settled in America and identified with the patriot cause.

But members of Congress were drawn to Washington's steadfast character. He was deliberate, solid, patient when he needed to be, wily at other times, and he learned from his mistakes (of which he was to make several on the battlefield). Unlike Adams and Franklin, he was not a quick wit, though he sometimes used earthy quips. He was not particularly religious, and, like most men, he appreciated flattery and disliked criticism. As a believer in colonial rights, he had shown himself neither a hothead nor a mouse. He was slow to anger, inspiring of trust, and not out for personal gain. Accepting the appointment, George Washington said he would accept no pay. He was commissioned to the command of the Continental Army on June 15, 1775.

Paul Revere

Thanks to Henry Wadsworth Longfellow's poem of 1863, Paul Revere's nighttime ride on the eve of the Revolution is an American icon. Yet the Boston silversmith's accomplishments far outweigh that deed. He took on management of a thriving silver shop at the age of 19, when his father died. After the Revolution, his son maintained the shop. An advertisement from 1787 indicates its variety of wares: tea and coffee urns, tankards, porringers, butter boats, mustard pots, tureen ladles, and sugar tongs.

A leader of the city's mechanic, or artisan, class when rustlings of revolution traveled through the streets of Boston, Revere helped organize American resistance efforts. Dressed as a Mohawk, he participated in the Boston Tea Party. As the main courier for Boston's Committee of Safety, he was assigned to carry news of patriot activity to New York and Philadelphia. On April 16, 1775, informed of approaching British troops, Paul Revere rode to Concord to warn locals to move their military stores. Two nights later, he and two other riders carried news to Lexington of British troop movement.

Narrowly avoiding capture as he set out, he was arrested between Lexington and Concord. An officer "clapped his pistol to my head," he wrote later, "and told me . . . if I did not give him true answers, he would blow my brains out." Released after the interrogation, he alerted John Hancock and Samuel Adams. If the British had followed him, they would have bagged Boston's two foremost agitators. During the war, Revere became a lieutenant colonel. He also engraved the first Continental money and drew political cartoons. After the war, he designed the official U.S. seal and cast the copper plate for the dome atop the Boston State House. In old age he cut a quaint figure around Boston, still wearing his Revolutionary-era garb.

A penny saved: Extolling liberty and virtue, the Massachusetts pine tree penny was designed and cast by Paul Revere in 1776. Because of a copper shortage, it never circulated, but it is often still considered the nation's original one-cent coin.

Once committed, Washington was never to give up. Like the other leaders of the Revolution, the man who became commander in chief was a rebel. In taking on this job he was staking everything he had—his life, his property, his liberty; he was likewise staking his reputation and honor, which he said he valued most highly. Persevering through seven long years of war, he came to symbolize the entire Revolution.

In Boston, people could not wait for a congressional decision. War had started, and now it was continuing on in several theaters simultaneously. For months, the statistical odds had appeared to be in Britain's favor. An army of 7,000 regulars—professional soldiers trained to fight with precision and well stocked with arms, ammunition, artillery, and money—stood against the Continental Army of American soldiers, about 16,000. Their superior numbers didn't matter, considering they were short-term enlistees, barely trained, supplied with a few captured artillery pieces, and financed with a currency based on good faith. Local and state militias were willing, but even less experienced and less reliable. And against the mighty Royal Navy the Americans could launch only privateers—merchant ships outfitted with guns, which might raid enemy commerce but could neither break the blockade nor move armies up and down the Atlantic coast, as British commanders did at will.

To advise Gage—or, more bluntly, to prod him to more vigorous action—three British generals arrived in Boston in May 1775: Sir Henry Clinton, who would wind up as commander at the end of the war; vainglorious John Burgoyne, a sometime playwright and bombastic stylist who called himself and his colleagues "the triumvirate of reputation"; and Sir William Howe, a brave soldier who preferred reconciliation to bloodshed. With Boston still besieged by patriots, the four British generals declared martial law. On June 13, they decided that within five days they would fortify a position on the mainland. The groundwork was laid for one of the bloodiest battles of the Revolution.

To beat the British to the punch, a patriot force of about 1,500 moved onto Charlestown peninsula, which jutted out into the Charles River just north of Boston. Under the command of valiant but untested Col. William Prescott, the patriot soldiers began digging earthworks—protective ridges, trenches, and windbreaks—on the night of June 16. Prescott must have either misinterpreted

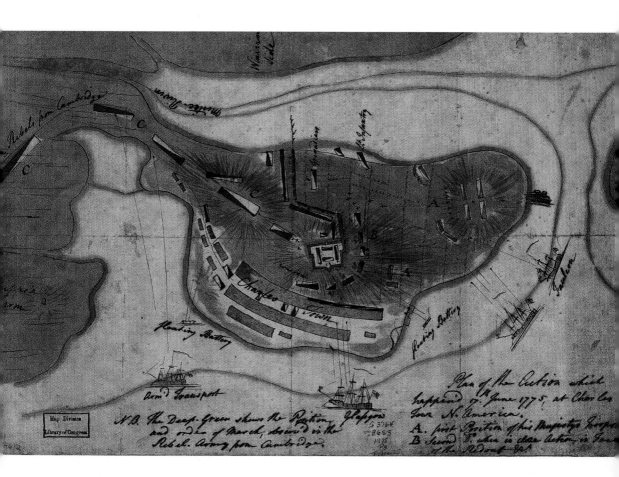

orders or decided, once he surveyed the scene, to change plans, because his detachment fortified Breed's Hill instead of the adjacent higher prominence, Bunker Hill.

Early the next morning, General Gage beheld the once-green knob of land now teeming with men. He called a meeting with the three newly arrived generals, who agreed that the patriot position must be attacked. Gage sent Howe with 1,500 men to the north side of Charlestown peninsula, where they could then march around and out-flank the patriot redoubt. But Howe got a late start, not landing on the peninsula until noon, and the patriots used that time to strengthen their position. Uncomfortable with the odds, Howe called for and received reinforcements.

Finally, Howe attacked the American left flank. An 18th-century battle was played out with a patterned formality that today seems both quaint and heartbreaking. Orderly ranks advanced in lines, drumbeats tapping their steps. When the opposing sides were within 15 paces—close enough to see expressions on the enemy's faces—the order to fire

Just after the Battle of Bunker Hill on June 17, 1775, British Gen. William Howe's aide-de-camp sketched this map of maneuvers. The British burned Charlestown, then advanced by water and land onto Breed's Hill. Howe claimed a victory but lost more than a thousand troops. "The success," he lamented, "is dearly bought."

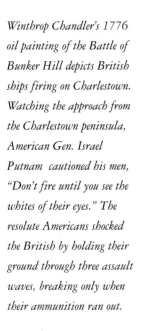

Winthrop Chandler's 1776 oil painting of the Battle of Bunker Hill depicts British ships firing on Charlestown. Watching the approach from the Charlestown peninsula, American Gen. Israel Putnam cautioned his men, "Don't fire until you see the whites of their eyes." The resolute Americans shocked the British by holding their ground through three assault waves, breaking only when their ammunition ran out.

Courtesy Museum of Fine Arts, Boston

was given. The soldiers massed tightly together in order to increase the odds that at least a few of their muzzle-loading muskets—not known for accuracy or dependability—had a chance of hitting targets. Even a highly trained redcoat could only manage to get off two or three shots in one minute's time. Muskets took time and care to reload, so those who had fired dropped back, and the next rank of artillerymen stepped forward. Between volleys, troops were wide open to a bayonet attack. Such warfare required constant drill and relentless discipline. The

British were superb at it. So when the redcoats advanced on Breed's Hill with bayonets gleaming, many a patriot volunteer must have had second thoughts.

As the British advanced up the hill in magnificent form, intending to teach the Yanks a lesson, the American officers cautioned their recruits to shoot first at the opposing officers, the ones with the shiny gorgets on their chests. In three ranks, the patriots let loose one devastating volley after another. The British were stunned.

The assault melted away and, at the bottom of the hill, Howe re-formed his lines and attacked again, bravely leading the charge. The same thing happened. Howe led a third assault, pouring in against the American redoubt. Up to now the Americans had had the momentum, but as they began to run out of ammunition, their luck changed. Having few bayonets to fight back with, the Yankees loaded and shot whatever they could find—nails, rocks, broken glass—then retreated.

Known ever after as the Battle of Bunker Hill, the day served as a lesson for the British. True, they had won a peninsula with some military advantage. Today Boston's Back Bay is a busy commercial neighborhood, but then it was all water: In revolutionary times, Boston was practically an island. By controlling Charlestown and hills to the north, the British kept a hold on the city. Still, the engagement on Bunker Hill, as Howe said, had proven an "unhappy day." American casualties numbered 450, about 30 percent of the 1,500 who fought, with 140 mortally wounded. More than 50 percent of the 2,200 British troopers fell—1,150, with 225 killed. The number of British officers killed and soldiers wounded at Bunker Hill was three times the average of all the 20 major battles of the war. Though the patriots left the field feeling defeated, they soon learned that their loss had delivered a big shock to the British.

A fortnight after the Battle of Bunker Hill, George Washington arrived to take up his post as commander of the new Continental Army. Reviewing his troops, he looked impressive on his horse, even to those who resented a Southerner coming to New England to take charge. He immediately set about the daunting task of trying to uniform and drill thousands of raw recruits into a cohesive fighting force.

LEAVING THE CONTINENTAL ARMY in Washington's care, we turn now to Canada, which Congress, exhilarated after Bunker Hill, had decided to invade. A lightning thrust into Canada, before Britain had a chance to send reinforcements, could win the territory of the neutral French Canadians to the patriot cause. If that were to occur, then Canada would join the rebellion as the 14th state—or so Congress hoped.

In May 1775, Benedict Arnold, a Connecticut apothecary, and Ethan Allen, the colonel of a Vermont militia called the Green Mountain Boys, had easily taken the fortresses at Ticonderoga and Crown Point, on Lake Champlain. These strongholds, bitterly fought over during the French and Indian War, lay along the strategic route linking Canada's St. Lawrence and New York's Hudson Rivers. Taking the fortresses seemed to open the way for an American attack on British forces in Montreal and Quebec. Congress believed that an American presence in Canada could persuade the French Canadians to take up arms against Britain and prevent the British from using Canada as a staging area to invade the rebellious colonies.

To assume command of the fortresses, Congress detailed Maj. Gen. Philip Schuyler. A native of Albany, Schuyler was a veteran of the French and Indian War and a delegate to the Continental Congress. A cautious man, Schuyler gathered men and supplies but remained skeptical that he had the forces to conquer and hold Canada. As the summer dwindled, the window of time for attacking Montreal narrowed. Schuyler was on leave in Albany when his second in command, Richard Montgomery, a handsome, Irish-born brigadier general, determined to go ahead with 1,200 men into Canada. Schuyler later joined him, then got sick and went back to Ticonderoga. With Montgomery in charge, the patriot force forged ahead, besieging Fort St. John on the Richelieu River. After 55 days the fort fell, and with it, the city of Montreal.

Meanwhile, a second American invasion force was approaching Quebec, trying to take that formidable fortress city before winter set in. Benedict Arnold was itching to win further glory. A couple of months before, in early September, Washington had given him the rank of colonel and deputized him to set off on a backdoor route to Quebec, with the idea that Arnold's and Montgomery's forces could converge on that city. Heading up the Kennebec River through the Maine woods, then portaging and scrambling to the Chaudière River and down to the St. Lawrence seemed like a good idea to those who glanced at the map. In fact, it was not.

The 35-year-old Arnold and his band of about a thousand men set out in November 1775 on an epic 45-day, 350-mile march to Quebec.

FOLLOWING PAGES: Cannons preside at Fort Ticonderoga, north of Albany, now rebuilt. On May 10, 1775, Americans led by Benedict Arnold and Ethan Allen captured the fort and the few British troops holding it.

For six torturous weeks, they fought the wilderness. Through dense woods, root-choked bogs, steep ravines, and waterfalls, they portaged loaded bateaux and waded in frigid chest-deep water. Snow, rain, and gale-force winds chilled the soldiers to their bones. Famished, many resorted to eating boiled moccasins, shot pouches, soap, and hair grease. They had to leave starving, drenched men to die.

The wonder is that they didn't all perish. One of the four divisions decided to turn back. Men belonging to the other three divisions were so depleted by death and sickness that only about 600 of them made it all the way. But their impetuous leader slogged on, and, with two-thirds of his original force, made it to the Plains of Abraham outside the French Canadian city. Pushed to the very limits of endurance, the human scarecrows who emerged from the wilderness had only a few weeks to catch their breath before they were asked to attack the citadel of Quebec.

By early December 1775, the combined forces of Arnold and Montgomery, numbering only about 1,000, laid siege to the walled city, defended by British and French troops less than 1,200 strong. The patriots opted to wait until the first snowstorm, to let it shroud an all-out attack. It finally came on the final day of the year—the last day of service for many men, since enlistment in the Continental Army lasted one calendar year.

Getting their forces to risk their lives in a blizzard on December 31, 1775 was itself an act of heroism on the part of Arnold and Montgomery—and a doomed one at that. In the first assault, Montgomery was shot dead, and his whole wing began to crumble. On the eastern side of the city, Arnold's forces rushed the streets, taking hits from men posted at loopholes. Arnold went down, wounded in the leg. "Don't give up!" he shouted, his blood painting the snow. "Go on boys! Go on boys!" Virginia rifleman Daniel Morgan picked up the column and made it to a final barricade. Unbeknownst to him, it was undefended, but he hesitated and thus lost his momentum. Soon he was surrounded and had no choice but to surrender.

In the failed siege of Quebec, the Americans lost half of their invading force. Most of the Americans fighting there were taken prisoner. The British tightened their hold when new regiments, strengthened by German mercenaries, crossed the Atlantic in the spring of 1776 and landed near Quebec. The surviving Yankees fell back on Montreal and then, in June 1776, their numbers further decimated by smallpox, they retreated again. They barely made it back to Fort Ticonderoga in the summer of 1776. Benedict Arnold was the last to leave Canadian soil.

Later on, France would ally with the American patriots, but in the winter of 1775 and 1776 it was, paradoxically, the French Canadians who saved Canada for Great Britain. Predominantly Catholic, they never joined the American cause. They deeply distrusted the Protestant Yankees, like Arnold, who in return denounced them and their so-called popery. Even after the war, American diplomats tried to obtain Canada as part of the peace negotiations that went on between the United States, Britain, and France. Had that plan succeeded, or had Quebec's 1,200 defenders failed, or even had Congress seen fit to send another 1,000 troops northward with Arnold, the borderlines of the United States might look different today.

But the American effort in Canada was far from pointless. It forced Britain to send army troops west to guard the St. Lawrence, thus dividing and weakening its forces, setting up the situation that led to crucial events at Saratoga nearly two years later.

The stately Château Frontenac Hotel dominates the skyline of modern Quebec. American forces led by Richard Montgomery and Benedict Arnold tried to take the citadel city in December 1775 but failed, their efforts weakened by smallpox, brief enlistments, and a lack of money.

As a Nation Is Born, so Are Its

hile the business of wresting a living from the land dominated life in early America, the colonists did enjoy the highest per capita income of anywhere in the world. Little wonder that they began developing a distinctly American culture, reflecting a self-reliant people discovering the beauties, facing the hardships, and interpreting the meaning of a new nation.

The earliest literary glimpses of America come from the

Arts and Its Culture

17th century. John Smith—English adventurer and governor of Jamestown, Virginia, in 1607 the first North American colony—spent his last years back in the Old World, writing books about the New, chief among them *The Generall Historie of Virginia, New-England, and the Summer Isles* (1624). William Bradford, one of the Pilgrims who traveled to Massachusetts on the *Mayflower,* kept a journal for more than three 17th-century decades, published in 1856 as *History of Plimoth Plantation.* Puritan leaders Cotton Mather, minister at Boston's Old North Church, and Jonathan Edwards, pastor in Northampton, Massachusetts, wrote sermons and tracts that form the spiritual foundation of American literature.

By the early 18th century, Philadelphia emerged as the colonies' cultural capital. Publisher and scientist Benjamin Franklin set the pace for American intellectual life. His earthy wit lent vigor to *Poor Richard's Almanack* (1733-1758) and his posthumous *Autobiography* (1791), publications that voiced the virtues that Americans came to claim as their own: thrift, industry, honesty, and public service.

Music filled the air in early America: chamber pieces from Europe, plain and solemn hymns, and rowdy tavern songs. Soon an American musical tradition emerged. Bostonian William Billings, a tanner by trade and friend to Samuel Adams and Paul Revere, wrote hymns and anthems such as those published in his *New-England Psalm Singer* (1770).

In visual art as well, a distinctive American style emerged as largely self-taught painters began to reflect the emerging nation on paper and canvas. The paintings of Gilbert Stuart, born in Rhode Island in 1755, now stand as national icons. He created striking portraits of the nation's first five presidents. Of the many likenesses he painted of George Washington, one was selected for the design of the one-dollar bill.

A portrait from around 1765, left, depicts children as miniature adults. Poet Phillis Wheatley, above, was brought to the colonies as a slave. In 1773, at 20, she became the first published African American with her Poems on Various Subjects, Religious and Moral.

In towns all over the new
nation, attentive crowds
heard the news.

Symbol of freedom, Philadelphia's Liberty Bell rang out on July 8, 1776, announcing the adopted Declaration of Independence. In use from 1753 until it cracked in 1841, the 2,080-pound bell is still ceremonially rung—that is, tapped—every Fourth of July. Its inscription comes from Leviticus: "Proclaim Liberty throughout all the land unto all the inhabitants thereof."

Chapter Three

In 1775, Americans believed they were fighting for their rights as British citizens. Connections with Great Britain were deeply ingrained in the fabric of Americans' private and public lives. Most Americans considered themselves loyal subjects of the crown, but they did not believe they should be governed directly by Parliament, where they had no representatives. They wanted to defend against what they saw to be threats and aggressive actions by British politicians, and they hoped that the king would come to their aid once he understood their plight. As the crisis deepened, debates heated up. Positions varied from acquiescence to compromise to outright separation, but—at least until 1776—independence was not the goal sought by most Americans.

Relations with France offered reasons to consider independence. As long as the conflict between America and Britain was simply a quarrel between colonies and the mother country, the French were not likely to risk intervening. But if the Americans decided to fight for independence from Britain, the outcome could be something that the French government deeply desired: Britain would lose valuable colonies and France would gain important commercial, perhaps even territorial, advantages. The American leadership began to realize that only if they fought for independence could they further their cause by winning an alliance with the French.

While an alliance was forming up between France and American insurgents, Britain was seeking foreign mercenaries to help put down the rebellion. When some of Germany's more impecunious princes heard that George III needed manpower to fight in the American colonies, they quickly offered to rent out soldiers. Altogether, nearly 30,000 troops were rented from German-speaking states. In one case, for example, soldiers in the service of the Duke of Brunswick were offered for a sum well beyond an average soldier's annual wages, to be paid to the duke upon the

PRECEDING PAGES: Congress commissioned John Trumbull, war veteran and friend to Washington, to paint The Declaration of Independence *in 1817.*

soldier's death, half if the soldier returned wounded. Since the principalities of Hesse-Cassel and Hesse-Hanau contributed the most men, the German mercenaries fighting in America were collectively referred to as Hessians. The patriots were particularly infuriated by Britain's hiring of mercenaries to put down the rebellion. Though it was common practice in those days, the use of foreign fighters, known for their brutality, heightened the American feeling that their king was turning against them.

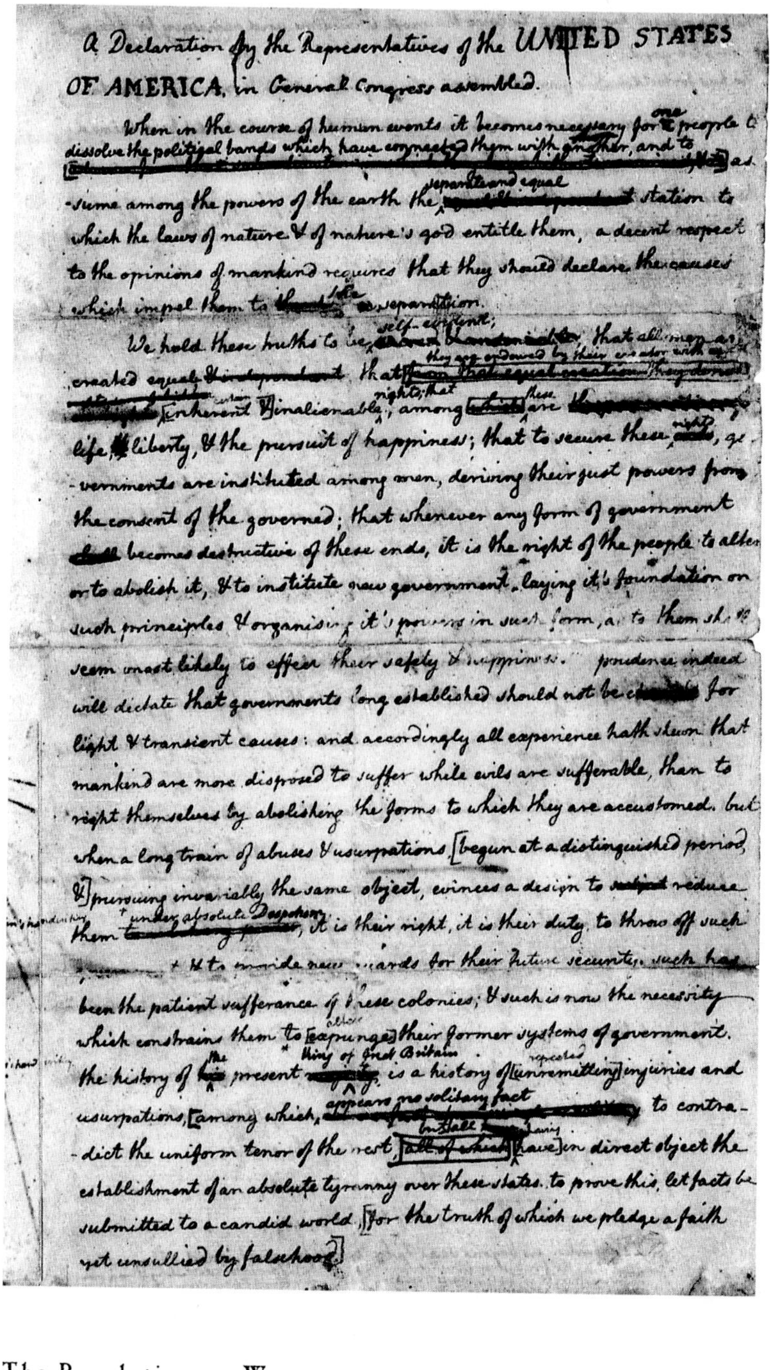

In 1776 Thomas Jefferson, a delegate to the Second Congressional Congress from Virginia, spent 17 days drafting the Declaration of Independence, shown here in his hand. Benjamin Franklin and John Adams edited it, then all delegates argued over every phrase.

The Revolutionary War

There were likewise instances in which British authorities dangled freedom before slaves, urging them to rise up against their owners. Such promises lured thousands of blacks from plantations, and these attempts at rousing domestic insurrection angered and frightened southern patriots. The British military also formed alliances with what Virginia lawyer and legislator Thomas Jefferson called "merciless Indian savages," leading to instances of frontier warfare that roused disgust and terror in patriot hearts.

By early 1776, it had become nearly impossible for most colonists to sustain the illusion of King George as a beneficent monarch who had simply been misled by Parliament. The publication in January of a remarkable 50-page pamphlet called *Common Sense* put barbed words to the thoughts and feelings of many Americans. In emotional language that ordinary people could understand, the English-born writer Thomas Paine cogently dismantled the whole idea of hereditary monarchy and advocated independence for the colonies. At best, he argued, government was "a necessary evil." England's kings were generally unworthy, and George III was a "royal ruffian." Rule by lineage should be abolished. "When we are planning for posterity," he wrote, "we ought to remember that virtue is not hereditary." Underlying his inflammatory rhetoric was the clear message, "We are not Englishmen; we are Americans!"

As a piece of political propaganda, *Common Sense* was brilliantly successful. Priced cheaply and frequently pirated, in just the first three months more than 100,000 copies of the pamphlet were purchased—the equivalent of one copy for every four or five adult males in America. The tract convinced many previously loyal Anglo-Americans that the only sensible course of action was complete separation from England. One by one that spring, colonies authorized representatives to call for independence at the Second Continental Congress.

At that meeting on June 7, 1776, Virginian Richard Henry Lee introduced three resolutions: He proposed the establishment of an American confederation. He called for an official attempt to gain European allies. And he called for a public proclamation "that these United States are, and of right ought to be, free and independent states, that they are absolved from all allegiance to the British crown, and that all political connection between them and the state of Great Britain is, and ought to be, totally dissolved."

That robust announcement would end up, almost word for word, in one of the most important documents in the history of the United States and the world: the Declaration of Independence. The five committee

To foil counterfeiters, Continental currency like this 18-pence note was sometimes issued with hard-to-imitate leaf prints. As the war dragged on, so much money was printed—and confidence in its future value dropped so low—that American currency became practically worthless.

FOLLOWING PAGES: Historic figures—here, William Penn—stand tall amid Philadelphia's modern buildingscape. A few blocks east of this view stands Independence Hall, seat of the Continental Congress and birthplace of the nation.

Toppling a monarch: A frenzied New York crowd reacted to the announcement of independence by pulling down a statue of King George III on July 9, 1776. Pieces of lead from the monument were sent to munitions makers and turned into 42,000 bullets.

members appointed to create the document agreed that Jefferson was the best writer and appointed him to draft the text. Curiously enough, statesmen of the time considered the issue of alliances more significant than the break with Britain. John Adams, appointed to both the proclamation and the alliance committees, took on drafting the proposed treaty and palmed off the job of writing a document declaring independence.

The 32-year-old planter-statesman assigned to write the draft came up with a remarkably forceful yet eloquent statement of the embryonic nation's hopes and ideals. Incorporating earlier resolutions, as well as political philosophy dating back to 17th-century English philosopher John Locke, the 1,817-word statement asserted that "all men are created equal," and that among the rights all were born with were "life, liberty, and the pursuit of happiness." It is interesting to note how Jefferson's now canonic phrases differ from sources he had at hand. His fellow Virginian, George Mason, penned that colony's Declaration of Rights, which stated that "all men are by nature equally

We have it in our power to begin the world over again.
A situation, similar to the present, hath not happened
since the days of Noah until now.

THOMAS PAINE, *Common Sense*, 1776

free and independent." And when John Locke listed intrinsic human rights, they included "life, liberty, and property." Jefferson's changes have provided fodder for generations of discussion and debate in classrooms and legislatures.

If a government violates the very rights it is supposed to protect, wrote Jefferson, then it is the duty of the governed to rebel. He backs up the claim of "abuses and usurpations" with 26 grievances against the King, building to an almost journalistic hyperbole: "He has plundered our Seas, ravaged our Coasts, burnt our towns, and destroyed the Lives of our People. He is, at this Time, transporting large Armies of foreign Mercenaries to complete the works of Death, Desolation, and Tyranny." As a result of these outrages, the colonies declared themselves severed from Britain, with the signers pledging "our lives, our fortunes, and our sacred honor." Members of Congress got a chance to hack at Jefferson's draft a bit. The author wasn't pleased by the cuts, but he was satisfied that his colleagues left it pretty much intact. One phrase condemning George III for condoning the slave trade was cut: The denunciation seemed hypocritical, but the text did retain the charge that the king was inciting slaves to rebel against their owners.

The decision to declare independence did not come easily. Some patriots—including, for example, John Dickinson of Pennsylvania—opposed the plan vehemently. Representatives from New Jersey, Maryland, and South Carolina argued against independence. Those in favor of it in Pennsylvania had to work outside existing governmental structures, organizing a pro-independence Pennsylvania Convention to counter the strong opposition in the Pennsylvania Assembly, led by Dickinson. On July 2, 1776, Lee's resolution passed by a vote of 12 colonies, with New York abstaining. John Adams predicted that the day would be forever celebrated. John Dickinson—no Tory, but a conservative who questioned the wisdom of an abrupt break from Britain—chose to miss the vote on July 4, when the Declaration itself, the formal document announcing the resolution, was adopted.

Jefferson kept his original draft—four handwritten pages. The text was sent to John Dunlap's Philadelphia printing shop that very night. By the next morning, riders were carrying broadside copies of the Declaration to various corners of the country, where colonial assemblies, committees of safety, and army officers read it aloud to gatherings. The news traveled as quickly as possible. British colonial authorities conveyed the word to London, although of course their messages had to travel across the Atlantic by sail. Two weeks after July 4 an official copy was engrossed, or printed, on parchment, and those available who had voted for it— along with some who hadn't—began to sign it in early August. When Congress retreated to Baltimore in December 1776, members took along the Declaration for safekeeping. In town squares all over the new nation, attentive crowds heard the news, and the United States hunkered down to the serious business of actually gaining its independence.

WHILE CONGRESS WAS ARGUING the merits of separating from the mother country, Britain's ships were advancing like furies to mete out punishment upon the errant child. Earlier in the year, William Howe had replaced Gage as commander of the British forces, and he was now converging on New York with 130 ships and 9,300 men. Taking control of America's main city, thought the British leadership, would dampen if not outright end the Revolution. By the second week in July, they were joined by Sir William's elder brother, Richard, Lord Howe, commander of the Royal Navy's squadron in North America. He arrived in New York, bringing from London an offer that he hoped would achieve reconciliation. If the American Congress would acknowledge Parliament's supremacy, the offer said, negotiations would begin. Congress refused to do so. The Howe brothers sincerely wanted to avoid war, but the ministry they represented back in London forced them into stances that provoked further conflict.

A month later, New York Harbor was white with sails. All told, 24,000 troops, both redcoats and German mercenaries, now massed on Staten Island, supported by 30 man-of-war battleships and nearly 400 transport ships—the largest overseas expedition ever undertaken by the British. Staten Island—then a barely inhabited backwoods region—became a British stronghold. At the little village of Brooklyn, on the western tip of Long Island, Washington ordered about one-third of his army of 28,000 to dig in and wait. Fearing a trap, he kept the rest on Manhattan. Many were inadequately armed and led. Few had any military experience beyond the Battle of Bunker Hill. Their task was to check the advance of the British into New York City.

With a population of 25,000, New York was a bustling port at the southern end of Manhattan Island. Stately three-story brick buildings and open-air markets graced the city's wide, tree-lined streets, which by 1776 had been built up no farther north than today's Canal Street. There, as the summer waned, the Howes continued building their forces. General Washington, moving about in and around New York City, inspecting his troops, was puzzled. Why would the Howes allow the patriots so much time to fortify the city? Washington was realistic. He did not expect to defeat the greatly superior British force, but only to inflict as much harm as he could. He would not leave New York without some kind of morale-building souvenir for his army. He exhorted his men to remember "that you are Freemen, fighting for the blessings of Liberty," and that "slavery will be your portion, and that of your posterity, if you do not acquit yourselves like men."

Sir William Howe held off on his campaign until he could be sure of victory. For one thing, a direct assault on New York might cause the Americans to flee and burn the city behind them, leaving no shelter for his troops. For another, he needed to root out the American

Thomas Jefferson

Statesman, diplomat, scientist, architect, horseman, violinist—Thomas Jefferson was all these and more. Unlike Washington, he was no military leader, and unlike Adams and Franklin, he was not a great speaker. But his wide-ranging intellect and powerful writing helped define American ideals.

In 1769, as a young lawyer, Jefferson was elected to the Virginia House of Burgesses; six years later, he was elected to the Continental Congress. Vehemently anti-British and a deft writer, Jefferson was a natural choice to draft the Declaration of Independence, which he considered, as he put it, "an expression of the American mind."

Shortly after the Declaration was adopted, Jefferson left Congress to return to Virginia. In 1779 he succeeded Patrick Henry as the state's governor. When, the British brought the war to Virginia in 1780, Jefferson proved himself unprepared for the military crisis. The redcoats forced the Virginia legislature to scatter. Jefferson was almost captured. In 1783 he survived an official investigation into his conduct and was elected to Congress. His years as President of the United States, from 1801 to 1809, sealed his enduring place among American heroes, but Jefferson wanted his tombstone to record three things: That he authored the Declaration of Independence, composed Virginia's Statute for Religious Freedom, and founded the University of Virginia, the nation's first state university.

artillery at Brooklyn Heights on Long Island, positioned to make British occupation of the city unfeasible. Just as Bunker Hill had been the strategic key to Boston, so Brooklyn Heights was paramount to controlling New York. Whichever side occupied the highlands effectively dominated the city below.

While the British were assembling their awe-inspiring force in New York Harbor in 1776, Gen. William Howe thought that extending the olive branch might save a lot of unnecessary trouble and bloodshed. Accordingly, on July 14 he wrote a letter to "George Washington, Esq." Washington refused to accept the letter, since Howe's address had not recognized Washington as a general. Howe dashed off another, this one to "George Washington, Esq., etc. etc.," claiming the "etc. etc." covered any possible titles. Washington took it as a further refusal to recognize Congress's authority to appoint him as head of the Continental Army. The two men did not meet.

Howe continued to plot and delay. When he finally put his plan into action, he did so methodically, and with devastating results. Unfortunately for the Americans, their stalwart leader on Long Island, Gen. Nathanael Greene, took ill on August 26, the night before the battle. Ultimately, though, this 34-year-old Rhode Island Quaker would become Washington's right arm.

In Greene's place, Washington appointed Gen. Israel Putnam, called "Old Put." A founder of the Connecticut Sons of Liberty, Putnam had fought roundly at Bunker Hill, but he often disagreed with Washington on tactics and ultimately proved unreliable. To make matters worse, since the Americans did not expect the attack to concentrate on Brooklyn Heights, they had not finished their defenses there. Thus, their left wing was exposed. Seeing this weakness, the British took swift advantage.

Howe had no intention of charging frontally, rank after rank, into the

Covered by the staunch First Maryland Regiment, patriots retreated across Gowanus Creek during the July 1776 Battle of Long Island. Gen. William Howe outflanked Washington and pushed him north to Manhattan. As John Adams wrote to his wife, Abigail: "In general, our Generals were out generalled." Still, Washington's masterful retreat saved 9,000 men and their equipment from capture.

American position, in the way that had brought on so much bloodshed at Bunker Hill. He massed some forces in front, meanwhile sending a shock force around to the east, through the back roads of Jamaica Pass, which a local Tory farmer reported as undefended. The thousands of patriot riflemen who had been posted in the woods to pick off the advancing enemy were thrown into confusion by this change in tactics.

The woods behind the marksmen were suddenly crawling with Hessians. Ordered not to shoot, they waited for the riflemen to fire, then charged with bayonets while the riflemen took time to reload. The carnage was horrendous—some men were stabbed as they ran away, others were speared to the trees they tried to hide behind. Giving little quarter, the Hessians chopped away until the screams of the vanquished

In 1776, forced to retreat across New Jersey, Washington's rookie troops took a severe beating in numbers and morale. The turnaround came, though, in early 1777: Victories at Trenton and Princeton let Americans advance over terrain through which they had recently retreated.

finally jolted the British officers into halting the blood work. More than 300 unburied corpses lay moldering in the "wood of horror," as it came to be called. Travelers a year later still complained of the smell. In local lore, the ghosts of that unquiet ground were not laid to rest for years.

Had General Howe promptly stormed the American entrenchments, he might have dealt a mortal blow to the Continental Army. Instead he bided his time, hoping that peace negotiations would end the battles. His men were exhausted, and the Americans, positioned on the edge of Long Island, were trapped between the British Army and the British fleet.

Howe's pause gave Washington just enough time to regroup. Thanks to the weather, the general's decisive action, and a couple of regiments of Massachusetts fishermen—led by the redoubtable Col. John Glover, a merchant and fisherman from Marblehead, Massachusetts—a rout was turned into a brilliant getaway. On the night of August 29, 1776, with the British lines a mere 600 yards from their position, the Americans left their fires burning and quietly slipped across the East River to Manhattan, where they joined the rest of Washington's army. A strong northwest wind made it impossible for British ships to enter the river that night, and a predawn blanket of fog cloaked the troops' movements. When the British realized what was going on, the last boat—with George Washington aboard—was just pushing off.

After the British drove Washington off Long Island, Congress appointed a committee to meet with the two Howe brothers. In early September 1776, off went three revolutionary representatives to the bargaining table: John Adams, Benjamin Franklin, and Edward Rutledge, a South Carolinian who had been educated at Oxford and admitted to the English Bar. The road from Philadelphia was so crowded with army stragglers, they had a hard time finding overnight accommodations. One night, Adams and Franklin shared one bed. Adams fell asleep listening to his bulky bedmate holding forth on the salubrious effects of fresh air.

After dining together on Lord Howe's flagship, the three got down to business with his lordship. They heard pretty much what they expected.

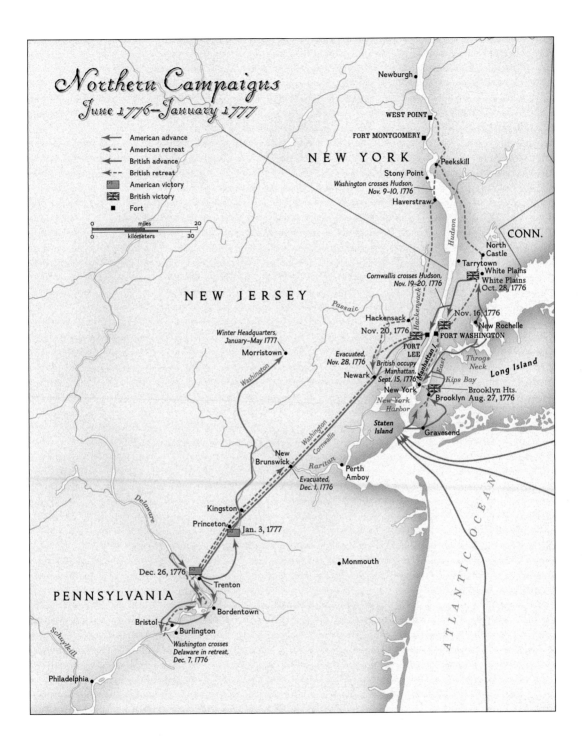

Northern Campaigns
June 1776–January 1777

American advance
American retreat
British advance
British retreat
American victory
British victory
Fort

miles 20
kilometers 30

NEW YORK

Newburgh

WEST POINT
FORT MONTGOMERY
Peekskill

Stony Point
Washington crosses Hudson,
Nov. 9–10, 1776
Haverstraw

CONN.

North
Castle
Tarrytown
White Plains
White Plains
Oct. 28, 1776

Cornwallis crosses Hudson,
Nov. 19–20, 1776

NEW JERSEY

Passaic

Hackensack
Nov. 20, 1776

Nov. 16, 1776
New Rochelle

FORT WASHINGTON

Winter Headquarters,
January–May 1777
Morristown

Evacuated,
Nov. 28, 1776

FORT
LEE

British occupy
Manhattan,
Sept. 15, 1776
Newark

Throgs
Neck

Long Island

Kips Bay

New York
New York
Harbor

Brooklyn Hts.
Brooklyn Aug. 27, 1776

Washington

Cornwallis

Staten
Island

Gravesend

Washington

New
Brunswick
Raritan
Perth
Amboy

Evacuated,
Dec. 1, 1776

Delaware

Kingston

Princeton
Jan. 3, 1777

Monmouth

Dec. 26, 1776

Trenton

PENNSYLVANIA

Bordentown

Bristol
Burlington

Washington crosses
Delaware in retreat,
Dec. 7, 1776

Schuylkill

Philadelphia

ATLANTIC OCEAN

Lord Howe had no authority to offer anything but a pardon and vague
assurances, couched in highfalutin language, that the colonies would be
treated fairly if the Americans would just quit fighting. He could not
even promise that Parliament would cease taxing the Americans. In short,

Despite smoking guns from forts on both sides of the river, British men-of-war were able to plow up the lower Hudson with little problem. In November 1776, forces under Gen. William Howe captured Fort Washington on the New York side, along with valuable materiel and nearly 3,000 prisoners. A few days later they crossed to New Jersey and took Fort Lee, scattering Washington's army south.

unconditional surrender was what he was asking. He said that he considered himself to be receiving the delegates as private gentlemen, not members of a congress his sovereign did not recognize. Adams retorted that he and his companions were happy to be received "in any capacity his lordship pleased, except in that of *British subjects*." "If America should fall," Lord Howe said, he would "feel and lament it like the loss of a brother." "We will do our utmost to save your lordship that mortification," Franklin replied. The conference soon ended, a failure, and Britain lost any chance to retain her colonies. The issues would have to be settled on the battlefield.

GEORGE WASHINGTON WAS DISAPPOINTED by his loss on Long Island, but his saving retreat gave him the reputation of a wily fox who could be as skillful in battle as any professional. He was by no means out of the woods, however, and he soon made a major mistake.

On September 7, 1776, Washington held a council of war with his generals to decide whether to try to hold New York, as Congress wanted, or to take the more prudent course and evacuate. With the generals evenly split in their opinions, Washington decided to try to do both— to hold and to move. He thus split his army, sending 9,000 troops to Harlem Heights in northern Manhattan, leaving 5,000 in the city, and scattering the rest in between. Only belatedly, on September 12, did he begin to concentrate his forces in the north.

Howe waited until the tides were right for a naval assault on Manhattan. He found his opportunity on September 15, before all the troops had moved north. British ships began bombing the Americans at one of their weakest points of defense: Kips Bay, on the east side of the island, near the site of the United Nations headquarters today. Soon an amphibious attack was underway. Young recruits bolted headlong before the terrifying din, leaving Washington only 80 yards from the approaching enemy. Bullets whizzing past, the general swore and lashed out with his riding crop, managing to rally his men and conduct an orderly retreat to Harlem Heights. Washington and his army barely escaped being trapped on Lower Manhattan, which could have been fatal for the cause of independence.

Later that day, the British marched into New York City without firing a shot. Most of the American forces had left. Once again, luck—and the failure of the British to capitalize on their momentum—saved the Continental Army from annihilation. As Howe moved into New York City, he looked forward to ample quarters for his army. For the most part, they were welcomed with open arms by a population more loyalist than patriot. But a few nights later a fire broke out, ultimately destroying about one-third of the city. New York remained British headquarters throughout the rest of the war, but in the fire's aftermath, living conditions were not so comfortable as Howe had expected.

Washington led his 4,000 dispirited men over New Jersey's muddy roads in the bleak retreat of November 1776. In a mere three months, the British had captured more than four thousand of his soldiers; daily desertions further weakened his force. Without new troops, he wrote his brother, "I think the game is pretty near up."

Washington was down to about 16,000 able-bodied men, against Howe's 25,000. But Washington now realized that it was not simply a matter of inferior numbers that was hurting his army. Until his soldiers got used to the roar of cannons, the smell of gunpowder, and the sight of bayonet charges, they would continue to panic and run. Molding them into a cohesive fighting unit was going to take time. Meanwhile, he opted for a policy of preserving as much of his army as possible rather than meeting the enemy in pitched battle.

In early October Howe resumed the offensive. He almost outflanked the Continentals by landing at Throg's Neck, on the southern tip of Westchester County, where a bridge now spans from the Bronx to Queens. Washington's forces barely managed to withdraw to central Westchester, hostile Tory country. Washington confronted Howe at White Plains on October 28 and suffered another humiliating withdrawal. He left about 3,000 men to guard Fort Washington, a primitive log-and-earth fortification established not long before in northern Manhattan, at a site near the east end of today's George Washington Bridge. Leaving troops there was another costly error.

Oswald, (des Generals Arnold letztheriger General-Adjudant) und Capitain Burr, welche zu Que-bec zu gefangenen gemacht wurden als der würdigste General Montgomery daselbst ein opfer der Ministerialischen rache wurde, jetzt an bord der Ministerialischen flotte zu Sandy-Hook sind.

Die rede gehet durchgängig, daß unsere kreuzfahrer 30 transportschiffe gegen Osten zu genommen haben.

Philadelphia, den 5 July.
Gestern hat der Achtbare Congreß dieses Vesten Landes die Vereinigten Colonien Freye und Unabhängige Staaten erkläret.

Die Declaration in Englisch ist jetzt in der Presse; sie ist datirt, den 4ten July, 1776, und wird heut oder morgen im druck erscheinen.

A German-American newspaper claimed the scoop: The first announcement of the country's severance with the motherland appeared in a July 5, 1776, edition of the Pennsylvanischer Staatsbote, *published in Philadelphia. "Yesterday," it reported, "the Honorable Congress of this Solid Land declared the United Colonies Free and Independent States."*

The Continental commander had not yet learned to trust his military instincts, which were telling him that Fort Washington was untenable and vulnerable to a siege. Its strategic position on the Hudson River made it extremely valuable, though, for harassing Britain's supply line into New York State. If the Americans could hold both Fort Washington and Fort Lee, across the river in New Jersey, they could string underwater obstructions between the two and block the British fleet from sailing up the deep Hudson River toward Albany. Washington had doubts about the Army's ability to hold Fort Washington, but he left the final decision to his trusted General Greene. Greene believed the fort could, and should, be held.

On November 16, the British attacked. Washington, across the river in Fort Lee, was helpless to do anything but watch. After a fearsome artillery barrage, Fort Washington's defenders looked through the smoke and saw a column of Scottish Highlanders, bagpipes skirling, escorted by Hessians with bayonets fixed. Many of the American soldiers panicked and ran for the river. The rest practically gave the fort away. The disaster was total: Only 150 Americans were killed or wounded, but more than 2,800 were captured, along with a bonanza of artillery, weapons, ammunition, tents, and equipment. And this time, the British did not relax.

They crossed the river into New Jersey and stormed Fort Lee on November 20. Washington and his troops barely made it out in time, along with a supply of gunpowder, but they left a horde of guns and other equipment behind. Retreating across the Hackensack River, Washington began hotfooting it southwest across New Jersey, the British dogging his steps. The New Jersey militia did not rally to the defeated general: On the contrary, hundreds of loyalists turned out in support of the crown.

With his forces now down to about 3,000 bone-weary troops, Washington fell back across the Delaware River into Pennsylvania on December 7, 1776. Before making camp, his men collected or burned all the boats for 75 miles along the river, so they could not be pursued. A remnant of the Continental Army remained in the Hudson highlands, about 50 miles north of New York City, to prevent Howe from moving up the river toward Albany. Most of the troops under Washington's command, though, were simply melting away.

Not accustomed to fighting in the cold months, and confident that they would wrap up the war in the spring, the British went into winter quarters. William Howe stationed himself through the cold months in New York, where he enjoyed glittering soirees, gambling sprees, and an American mistress. For the time being, he saw little point in continuing to chase a ragamuffin army across the countryside.

On the patriot side, spirits had never been lower. But Washington was not quite ready to say that 1776 was over.

Fog shrouds the Delaware River Valley, across which Washington retreated in late 1776. With enlistments expiring soon, Washington watched his army dwindle: "You may as well attempt to stop the Winds from blowing," he wrote, "as the Regiments from going when their term is expired."

The Power of the Printing Press

*T*he newspapers! Sir, they are the most villainous—licentious—abominable—infernal—Not that I ever read them—no—I make it a rule never to look into a newspaper." So claims a character in *The Critic,* a play by Richard Sheridan, England's leading playwright of the 1770s. For readers in Britain, the news from America, at least from their point of view, was generally bad.

While British newspapers were taking jabs at their own nation's war efforts, American newspapers were busy fanning the fires of anti-British feeling. Journals published in port cities like Boston, New York, and Philadelphia made their way by boat and horse to news-hungry readers in colonial villages.

With literacy steadily increasing and life-altering events occurring regularly, the American press flourished in the late 18th century.

In such turbulent times, the reporting could often be biased. After Patrick Henry's fiery, near-treasonous speech against the Stamp Act, legislators passed the Virginia Resolves, declaring that Virginians could be taxed only by Virginians. But Joseph Royle, publisher of the *Virginia Gazette,* was too Loyalist to print the final version. Unfortunately for his cause, an earlier, more inflammatory version of the Resolves was printed by the *Newport Mercury,* stirring other colonies to action. In 1775 the offices of the *New-York Gazetteer,* a paper that tried to present both sides of the issues, were destroyed by the Sons of Liberty, who hanged the publisher in effigy.

It was not only men who wielded the power of the press. Of about forty colonial newspapers, as many as six were published by women. Sarah Updike Goddard and her daughter, Mary Katherine, both published Baltimore newspapers in the 1760s and '70s,

in a Time of Revolution

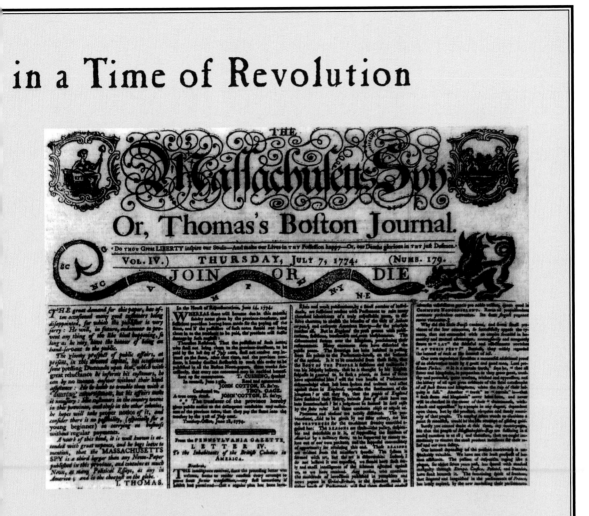

at a time when paper itself was often difficult to come by.

After the war was over, but before the Constitution had been drawn up, Thomas Jefferson underscored the importance of a free press when he wrote, "The basis of our government being the opinion of the people, the very first object should be to keep that right; and were it left to me to decide whether we should have a government without newspapers, or newspapers without a government, I should not hesitate a moment to prefer the latter."

From the first days of the Revolutionary War on, Americans depended on the power of their press. Since 1791, the First Amendment to the Constitution has protected that freedom.

A rattlesnake, above, emblem of the 13 colonies, ornamented the masthead of The Massachusetts Spy. *Benjamin Bannaker's almanac, opposite, published from 1791 to 1802, was one of the most popular of its day.*

*No matter how many battles the
British had won, the Americans still
would not concede.*

American flags wave at Washington Crossing State Park, where a tattered army pulled itself together and crossed the Delaware to take Trenton, New Jersey. In the process, American soldiers regained their morale and reversed the course of the war. But for Washington's gamble, the epitaph of the entire Continental Army might have been inscribed here.

Chapter Four

O n the west side of the Delaware River, in mid-December 1776, Gen. George Washington pondered his situation. The Continental Congress had fled Philadelphia for the safer confines of Baltimore, giving him full discretionary power to carry on the war as he saw fit. His troops were battered, their esprit de corps at a low ebb. At the end of the month, most of the men's one-year enlistments would expire, further reducing a force already weakened by desertion, capture, and casualty. Across the river, Howe had positioned 3,500 Hessians at Trenton and Bordentown. He wanted to make the Americans think twice about taking the offensive during the winter, although he seriously doubted they would. The Hessian commanders considered their enemies almost beneath contempt, and as the days wore on and cold weather set in, they practically forgot them.

On December 19, 1776, a pamphlet appeared on the streets of Philadelphia, containing an essay that had the effect of a minor miracle. Thomas Paine, the author of *Common Sense,* had been traveling with the American Army, and General Washington had enjoyed his company. Paine had told the general he would try to write something to help the troops, and he fulfilled his promise by writing the first issue of *The Crisis,* a series of political and philosophical essays published as inexpensive pamphlets over the next 15 months.

When Washington read Paine's words, he was transported. He ordered copies sent and read to all the brigades. Up and down the river, Paine's words of revolution, bravery, and hope echoed, rousing the troops to believe in the cause for which they were fighting:

> *These are the times that try men's souls. The summer soldier and the sunshine patriot will, in this crisis, shrink from the service of his country; but he that stands it now, deserves the love and thanks of man and woman.*

PRECEDING PAGES: *With Washington upstage, John Trumbull's painting of the Battle of Princeton captures the never-say-die spirit of the Continental Army.*

These words, now scripture in the mythology of early America, helped many a man that day gird for whatever lay ahead.

Washington began working on a daring plan that could mean disaster for his dwindling army. He would take his men back across the river and launch a surprise attack on the Hessians. To see how the idea would fly with others, he met with the highly respected Gen. Horatio Gates, a British-born soldier soon to prove better behind a desk than in the field.

Washington proposed dividing his men into three brigades. Leading one brigade, he himself would cross the Delaware River nine miles north of Trenton and march south into the town, where Hessian forces made their encampment. The second brigade would cross just below Trenton. The third would cross about fifteen miles south of Trenton, march north, and attack the Hessians at Bordentown. Gates—usually cautious, and at times even overcautious—said the whole plan sounded foolhardy and left the next day for Philadelphia with his aides. In Gates's absence, Washington ordered Gates's 500 men to remain in camp. To his fellow officers, Washington reported that Gates was sick and had to leave. Then Washington went ahead with his plan. On the night of December 24, he and his officers met in a farmhouse to go over final plans for the attack. They studied maps and synchronized watches.

It was cold and rainy on Christmas morning, and on the east side of the Delaware, the Hessians feasted and drank and sang. By evening it had begun to snow, softly at first, and then harder, slanting in a freezing wind. The Hessian pickets had been told to stay alert, but they did not expect any action. Garrison commander Johann Rall, the Hessian colonel who had accepted the American surrender of Fort Washington, went to bed drunk.

When darkness fell, the scene on the other side of the river was altogether different. In a swirl of activity and orders, Washington loaded the first men and a few pieces of artillery for the crossing. The taciturn, pinch-faced John Glover and his Massachusetts fishermen, who had saved Washington on Long Island, might have been tired of the war, but they were rock-solid reliable. Glover had rounded up heavy, wooden Durham boats for the attack. Used for hauling iron, these sturdy, canoe-shaped craft, 50 feet long, could hold 40 people. But with hundreds of men crossing, many still had to wait their turn. Hard-knuckled fishermen poled the boats, full of troops, across the river through the driving snow and sleet, pushing ice floes out of the way. Not until four in the morning had all the soldiers made it across. With nine miles to hike on muddy roads in the dark, a predawn sneak attack was now impossible.

$\mathcal{B}$e courteous to all, but intimate with few,
and let those few be well tried
before you give them your confidence.

GEORGE WASHINGTON, IN A LETTER TO HIS NEPHEW, BUSHROD WASHINGTON, 1783

Washington's men set out anyway, some with no shoes, slipping in the icy mud, trying but failing to keep their gunpowder dry. They now called their campaign "Victory or Death"—a password given by Washington himself for all those engaged in the operation. They did not yet know that the commander of one of the other brigades, farther down the river, had decided it was too ice-choked to cross, or that the commander of the other would cross, change his mind, and cross back.

Washington's brigade arrived at the Hessian pickets at nearly eight o'clock, but a misty rain kept visibility low. Two young soldiers rode eagerly forward: Capt. William Washington, a distant relative of the general, and Lt. James Monroe, later the nation's fifth president. Swords drawn, they silenced the sentry before he could spread the alarm. This was the kind of moment these two dashing young officers lived for, and they played it perfectly, cutting down the sentry and scattering the guards before any one could reach his musket. Then Washington's exceptional young aide, Alexander Hamilton, helped bring up the heavy guns.

In town, half-awake Hessian soldiers were stumbling from their billets, trying to form up ranks. Rall, roused from his bed, came wheeling out into the streets on horseback, ordering his men to advance. One of the few Continental riflemen with dry powder took careful aim and hit Rall. Soldiers fought savagely, house to house, but with their commander mortally wounded, the resistance efforts of the Hessians collapsed, and the Battle of Trenton was over in just an hour. About one third of the Hessian soldiers escaped, but more than 100 were killed and more than 900 were taken prisoner. On the American side, a couple of soldiers died of hypothermia, and those were the only losses.

After his troops withdrew across the Delaware, Washington worked hard to convince them to stay in service beyond the turn of the year. Writing in 1832, a soldier recalled how in late December 1776, Washington implored his troops to keep fighting. "The General wheeled his horse about," as the veteran recalled it more than half a century

FOLLOWING PAGES:
Students take in the art of war in New York's Metropolitan Museum of Art. Emanuel Leutze's famous 1851 painting, Washington Crossing the Delaware, *is not accurate, yet the painting drives home the resolute spirit of the Americans.*

A few days after his stunning victory at Trenton in late 1776, Washington was on the warpath again, this time at Princeton. In a cunning feint-and-circle maneuver, the American commander left Cornwallis facing an empty campsite while he captured Princeton, thereby retaking most of New Jersey in an 11-day trail of glory.

later. General Washington rode back to face the men in his regiment and said:

> My brave fellows, you have done all I asked you to do, and more than could be reasonably expected; but your country is at stake, your wives, your houses and all that you hold dear. You have worn yourselves out with fatigues and hardships, but we know not how to spare you. If you will consent to stay only one month longer, you will render that service to the cause of liberty and to your country which you probably never can do under any other circumstances.

The follow-up to the Battle of Trenton was rash, surprising, and brilliant. Washington gathered a force of 5,000 men. Sir William Howe, incensed by the fall of Trenton, shipped out a force of 6,000, led by 38-year-old Charles, Lord Cornwallis. A member of Parliament who had argued against the Stamp Act, Cornwallis had proven battle-worthy during the Seven Years' War in Germany. By 1776 he had reached the rank of major general. After participating in the action at Fort Washington and Fort Lee, Cornwallis took command of British troops at Trenton, little knowing the role he was to play in American history.

The Revolutionary War

Washington and Cornwallis's forces sparred near Trenton, New Jersey, on January 2, 1777, but it was late in the day, and Cornwallis decided to pull back until morning. Washington knew he was in grave danger, pitted against the brash British general. On the other hand, he could not retreat across the river without heavy losses. Leaving campfires burning, the fox quietly slipped from the hole again, taking his men south, then east, and around the British camp. As he awoke the next morning, Cornwallis was shocked to hear gunfire coming from Princeton, several miles to his rear. In retreating, Washington had decided to attack. He routed three British regiments, took over the town of Princeton, and gained a goodly cache of guns and supplies. He then considered pushing on to New Brunswick, but decided to quit while he was ahead. His dog-tired men had done enough.

Heading to the safety of the hills up around Morristown, New Jersey, 45 miles west of New York City, Washington could finally breathe a sigh of relief. His valiant little force had taken back much of New Jersey. They ended the year on a high note. In just over a week, the Continental Army had turned its fortunes completely around. They had proved to themselves that they could fight, and win.

AFTER TWO YEARS OF WAR, the British were growing frustrated. It did not seem to matter how many battles they had won; the Americans still would not concede. The British kept slamming them, but the Americans kept coming back for more. You could practically grab them in your hands, but they would slip away like water and regroup somewhere else. In faraway London, the British government decided to refocus attention on Canada and try an invasion from the north. British Gen. John Burgoyne was assigned to the mission.

At 53 years of age, "Gentleman Johnny" Burgoyne was older than Howe and Clinton, the other two generals with whom he had arrived in 1775, although he was their junior in rank. He was flamboyant, full of bluster, a gambler, and he had a flair for the dramatic—he was, in fact, the author of numerous plays. He deemed the American stage a good place to win lasting glory, and thus he politicked behind the scenes to get himself appointed over Sir Guy Carleton, governor of Canada, as commander of an army that would march south from Canada to Albany. Burgoyne had never before held independent command, nor did he have a glimmer of the difficulties awaiting him in the forests of New York. His name is indeed remembered, but not in the way that he had hoped.

The plan was for Burgoyne to march an army down the Lake

John Burgoyne

One of the most colorful leaders fighting against the Americans during the Revolution, Gen. John Burgoyne served with distinction in the Seven Years' War after his father-in-law, the Earl of Derby, purchased him a captaincy. Burgoyne was elected to Parliament in 1761 and promoted to major general in 1772.

Nicknamed "Gentleman Johnny" because he was so kind to his soldiers, Burgoyne was also an inveterate gambler, an amateur actor, and a capable playwright. His first major play, *Maid of the Oaks,* starred London's beloved actor, David Garrick, in 1774. Soon thereafter, in 1775, the flamboyant general arrived in America with Generals Howe and Clinton, all three sent to serve the British cause.

Through the tedious months of military stalemate in the early years of the war, Burgoyne penned a farce titled *The Siege of Boston.* During its performance in Charlestown, near Boston, the actor playing George Washington had just taken the stage when a British sergeant burst into the theater, yelling, "The Yankees are attacking Bunker's Hill!" The pro-patriot audience applauded, at first believing the line to be part of the play.

In the summer of 1777 Burgoyne launched an ill-fated invasion of New York from Canada. After capturing Fort Ticonderoga, his army bogged down along the Hudson River. Facing an American force commanded by Gen. Horatio Gates and more than three times the size of his own, Burgoyne surrendered his entire army at Saratoga. His military failure earned him severe criticism at home. Three years later, he published *A State of the Expedition from Canada,* a campaign account that explained his actions.

After the American Revolution, Burgoyne's fortunes shifted according to the party in power in Great Britain. He served briefly as commander in chief in Ireland in 1782, but soon retired from military service. His most famous play, *The Heiress,* a light drama about class and inheritance, ran successfully in London in 1786. In a liaison with a London singer, Burgoyne fathered four illegitimate children. He died suddenly in 1792, and in death, he garnered honors: He is buried in Westminster Abbey.

Champlain–Hudson River route to Albany and isolate New England, perhaps with cooperation from Howe, who was more interested in taking Philadelphia and smashing Washington's army. The British generals didn't fuss over the plan in much detail: They were not accustomed to thinking in terms of such endless tracts of wilderness. It was enough in the spring of 1777 that they had some sort of plan of action.

From the beginning, the operation developed flaws. Not happy playing supporting actor to Burgoyne, Howe protested to Lord George Sackville Germain, secretary of state for the colonies, directing war maneuvers from London. Howe complained that his troops needed to be available farther south. Germain agreed to let him act independently, and to move north when he thought best. There was now no central command. The armies might meet, or they just might not.

IN THE MIDDLE OF JUNE, Burgoyne's army of more than 7,000 British and German troops began heading south from Fort St. John, near Montreal. Accompanying this force were several hundred French Canadians, Tories, and Indians, as well as a large contingent of soldiers' wives and other women who cooked, cleaned, and nursed the sick and wounded. No motley mob, this army was composed of the finest British and Hessian officers and fighting men, their weapons polished as they marched, then floated in bateaux up Lake Champlain, with bands lending an air of martial gaiety. They kept their uniforms as tidy as possible, although a ship bringing replacement uniforms from England had been seized by a privateer. Patches had to be cut from their coattails. The Germans among them had to march without their customary thigh-length jackboots and elbow-length leather gauntlets, but their hats were still topped with fine, tall feathers.

In the meantime, Lt. Col. Barry St. Leger, a British officer who had fought in the French and Indian Wars, was marching eastward from Fort Ontario to join Burgoyne's forces. St. Leger's troops, numbering less than a thousand in total, included some Native Americans. Distressed at the encroachments of American settlers, most of the six Iroquois nations—Indians who lived in what is now upstate New York—sided with the British during the Revolution. Germain claimed that white officers would always see that Indians fought appropriately, but the British knew that scalping and other atrocities would inevitably occur.

Burgoyne seized on locals' fears by issuing a proclamation filled with literary fustian. He warned the Americans who continued this "unnatural rebellion" that thousands of Indians would be loosed upon them, and

Knowing that Howe and his redcoats were encamped in Germantown, five miles north of Philadelphia, Washington attempted a complicated military action on October 4, 1777. Some 120 British soldiers took shelter in a large stone house belonging to Benjamin Chew, Pennsylvania's chief justice. One American column got lost in the all-day fog, others wasted time besieging the Chew house. Their plans gone awry, the Americans finally retreated.

that he himself would "stand acquitted in the eyes of God and man" for what the warriors would do "in the phrenzy of hostility." The Americans must give in or look forward to "devastation, famine, and every concomitant horror that a reluctant but indispensable prosecution of military duty must occasion." The bombastic threat just steeled patriot resolve, and it was not well received in London. One critic labeled Burgoyne "Pomposo," and Lord North howled with laughter.

Nevertheless, Burgoyne rolled south without trouble, arriving at Fort Ticonderoga, on the upper, or south, end of New York's Lake Champlain,

The Revolutionary War

on June 30, 1777. The British considered Ticonderoga the "Gibraltar of America," since its strategic position represented control of and access to the St. Lawrence–Hudson waterway. With that analogy, though, they overestimated its importance: In the vast American wilderness, control of such a waterway, via Ticonderoga, did not equal the same military power that control of Gibraltar might in the Mediterranean.

The British began with the upper hand, though, and pressed on to control Ticonderoga. In consultation with Philip Schuyler, commander of America's northern army, Maj. Gen. Arthur St. Clair took the lead. St.

Among the engines of war were bullet molds, such as this embossed soapstone piece. The mold was heated over a fire, molten lead poured into the troughs, and the two halves pressed together. Cooled bullets had a sprue, or lead stem, easily trimmed off with a jackknife.

Burgoyne's savages, opposite, are portrayed as mercilessly dispatching a helpless frontier woman—and that's how the murder and scalping of Jane McCrea played in the patriot press, never mind that she was engaged to a Tory lieutenant. McCrea's death in July 1777 fueled Patriot anger and swelled militia ranks just before the Battle of Saratoga.

Clair, born in Scotland, had settled in Pennsylvania and fought under Washington in the Battle of Trenton. He fended off the British as long as possible. American forces at the fortress were few. St. Clair estimated that he needed at least 10,000 men to hold Ticonderoga—he had barely 2,000. Furthermore, in fortifying the area, the Americans had left the adjacent Sugar Loaf Hill untouched, believing that it was impossible to haul artillery up its rugged flanks. Burgoyne's chief engineer and artillery general assessed the situation. They agreed that they could clear a path up the hill and have cannons at the top in 24 hours. On the morning of July 5, St. Clair and his officers saw artillery staring down at them. Now they knew there was no way they could keep Ticonderoga.

That night the Americans evacuated the fort. Their movements were almost given away by a fire, set accidentally by a French officer serving with them, who knocked over a candle while awakening from his drunken stupor. The next morning Burgoyne found himself in possession of Ticonderoga, with the Americans in full flight. The rest of the campaign, he thought, would be even easier. When George III heard the news, a few weeks later, he crowed, "I have beat them! I have beat all the Americans!"

There were now only about 70 miles separating Burgoyne from his goal of Albany. But once he departed from Lake Champlain, heading to the Hudson River by way of Skenesboro—now Whitehall, New York—he found himself in one mess after another. Instead of a straight road south, the way was a twisting, up-and-down trail over slick creeks and through devilishly thick woods. Within this nearly impenetrable wilderness, the army had to drag scores of heavy artillery and other gear, all with insufficient horsepower. To make it even more of a trial, American woodsmen seemed able to keep always a step ahead of them, chopping down great numbers of trees to block the path, diverting streams, and turning dry ground into swamps. Burgoyne's men contended as best they could with these obstacles, but it ended up taking more than three weeks just to go the 35 miles to Fort Edward on the Hudson River, halfway to Albany.

Burgoyne went a few miles farther south, to Fort Miller, then waited several weeks for all his artillery to be brought forward. His situation grew ever more precarious the longer he sat. His supply line was stretched as thin as a capillary and was constantly harassed by patriot skirmishers. American troops did not realize how bogged down the British were. Schuyler, cautious and lackluster in 1775, sent pessimistic reports to

The Revolutionary War

*J hope . . . that mankind will at length . . . have reason
and sense enough to settle their differences without cutting throats;
for in my opinion, there never was a good war, or a bad peace.*

BENJAMIN FRANKLIN, IN A LETTER TO JOSIAH QUINCY, 1773

Philadelphia and kept retreating, until he was south of Saratoga near
the mouth of the Mohawk River. Finally, on August 4, Congress relieved
the stodgy leader of his command, replacing him with Horatio Gates.

Desperate for food, horses, and wagons, Burgoyne sent out a raiding
party southeast to Bennington, in the Green Mountain country of western New Hampshire, now Vermont. Lt. Col. Friedrich Baum, a German
mercenary officer, led 700 men into the countryside, brushing off patriot
resistance. But when he reached Bennington, he encountered a force of
2,000 militia, raised up by a tall, plucky 49-year-old rifleman named
John Stark, a brigadier general from New Hampshire and a veteran of
Trenton and other battles.

Stark had little trouble rounding up men eager to fight, because at the
end of July, some of Burgoyne's Indians had murdered a woman named
McCrea, the fiancée of a loyalist fighting on the British side. The story
had leapt through the grapevine and the patriot press, growing in
horror, until Burgoyne became a demon who could not or would not
control his savages.

On August 16, while Baum waited for backup, Stark attacked. He
soon had the invaders in a vise. A fierce two-hour battle ensued, at times
hand-to-hand. Finally Baum was mortally wounded, and his troops ran
or surrendered. By the end of the day, the patriots had reduced Burgoyne's
army by some 900 soldiers—a tenth of the total—at a cost of only 70
casualties. Adding to his plight, Burgoyne learned that St. Leger had
been sent packing by Benedict Arnold at Fort Stanwix, one hundred miles
west. Arnold's clever false report that he had 3,000 men (instead of the
1,000 he really had) tricked St. Leger's Indians into quitting.

WHILE BURGOYNE LOST MEN TO BATTLE, illness, and desertion, Gates
was gaining men all the time. By early September, Burgoyne made the
fateful decision to cross the Hudson and try to fight his way down to
Albany. Now there was no question of his retreating and saving his
dwindling army—it was either prevail, or go down in flames.

The Revolutionary War

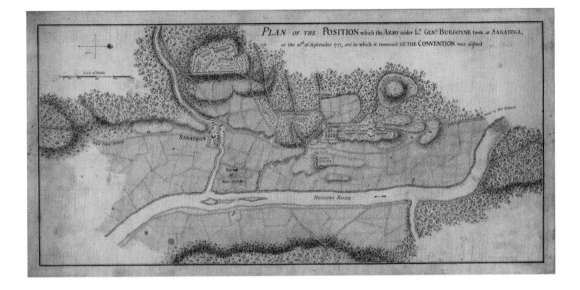

PLAN OF THE POSITION which the ARMY under LT GENL BURGOYNE took at SARATOGA, on the 10th of September 1777, and in which it remained till THE CONVENTION was signed

Horatio "Granny" Gates—nicknamed for his concern for his troops and his unmilitary-looking spectacles—was no genius of the battlefield. But now, in the fall of 1777, the heavens aligned to bless him, if he could just take advantage of the gift. He had cautious instincts and, based on his experience as a British-trained professional soldier, he thought that American forces could win only if they stood behind well-entrenched positions. From there, they could force the redcoats, outnumbered by the patriots, to attack.

At the beginning of September Gates moved his army about 25 miles north of Albany, to a place called Bemis Heights. There the Hudson flows past high bluffs a few hundred yards west of the river. Under those bluffs passed the only road to Albany, affording very little room to maneuver. It was the perfect place for Gates's army to entrench and dare Burgoyne to fight on Yankee terms. Thaddeus Kosciuszko, a Polish military engineer who had volunteered to serve the American cause, and Benedict Arnold, just back from relieving Fort Stanwix, found the spot to make the stand. Kosciuszko's fieldworks gave the Americans an impregnable position, effectively blocking Burgoyne's way. All Gates had to do now was wait for what he knew "Gentleman Johnny" Burgoyne would do: attack.

And on September 19, attack he did. On a clearing atop Bemis Heights called Freeman's Farm, Burgoyne tried to outflank the Americans to the west, but after a terrific struggle, his redcoats and German mercenaries had to fall back. They had not reached Kosciuszko's entrenchments. At the end of the day, American losses

Contrary to its inscription, this period map actually shows the village of Saratoga, current-day Schuylerville, where Burgoyne surrendered in October 1777. The "Battle of Saratoga" was actually two battles, which took place on a farm about ten miles south. The campaign was named for the nearest town, leading to confusion among early chroniclers.

Gracious in victory, Gen. Horatio Gates, at left, received and then returned the sword of defeated Gen. John Burgoyne at Saratoga on October 17, 1777. Said Burgoyne, "The fortune of war, General Gates, has made me your prisoner."

numbered about 300, British and German losses twice that. Major credit for the American success went to Benedict Arnold and Daniel Morgan, who had also fought together so bravely at Quebec.

Burgoyne could not afford to keep losing troops. He fortified his encampment on Bemis Heights, licked his wounds, put his men on half-rations, and waited for relief from Sir Henry Clinton. Clinton, though, was far away in New York City, having sent only a small force up the Hudson. They had turned back at Kingston. Burgoyne had

given up on Howe, who was just now entering Philadelphia, only to find that the Congress had vacated the city.

Without his Indian scouts, Burgoyne was operating blind. The only way he could communicate with the outside world was through a few Tory horsemen. One hid his message by swallowing it. Americans captured him, forced him to disgorge the capsule, and hung him as a spy. On October 7, 1777, Burgoyne decided again to try to ram his way through the woods west of the American line. The second battle on Bemis Heights was underway.

Fiery Benedict Arnold had quarreled with Gates, who had omitted his name from the report on the first battle that he had written for Congress. As a result of their quarrel, Arnold was removed from command. But now, seeing Burgoyne attempting to outflank the patriots, Arnold thrust himself back in the fray. Full of wild energy, he yelled courage into his men and led one unit after another in death-defying assaults on the enemy. Ultimately his horse was killed under him and his leg was shattered by a German musket shot.

The fight ended in a crushing defeat for Burgoyne. It was a resounding victory for the Americans over some of the world's best professional troops. The raw courage of half-trained Continentals and untrained Yankee militia, the inspirational battlefield leadership of Arnold, Morgan, and several other generals—not including Gates himself—and the superbly designed American fieldworks had combined to send Burgoyne down to a defeat that would resonate across the Atlantic.

As Burgoyne withdrew to the village of Saratoga, about eight miles to the north, Gates sent out militia to seal off all possible exits. Militiamen flocked in, swelling the American force to more than 17,000, while the ranks of the British and Germans dwindled below 5,000—and they were hungry. On October 12, Burgoyne finally decided to retreat to Canada, but it was too late. He was surrounded.

On the following day, October 13, 1777, Gates demanded surrender. After some negotiation, Burgoyne said his troops would lay down their arms and pledge never to fight in America again if they could then sail back to England. Gates agreed, and on October 17 Burgoyne's men respectfully grounded their arms in front of the Americans, in adherence to standard military protocol. When they were out of sight, Burgoyne gracefully tendered his sword to Gates. A few days later, Burgoyne finally made it to Albany—as a prisoner. Respect for his rank and reputation was duly expressed: General Schuyler invited him to dinner, and with a gracious wave of his hand dismissed the British burning of his country home at Saratoga.

The offer of terms for surrender turned out to be a mere formality. The British and German prisoners were never allowed to return to their homes across the Atlantic. Neither Washington nor Howe was satisfied with the Saratoga convention—both felt cheated by earlier prisoner exchanges and were looking for ways to recoup. Howe planned to reenlist the soldiers, but they were sent off to prisoners' quarters before he had a chance. Washington did not want them to go home and replace garrison soldiers, who would then be shipped out for more fighting in America. Most of the imprisoned soldiers died before the war had reached an end. Those who survived remained in America and blended into the population.

The loss of Burgoyne's entire army at Saratoga—the worst defeat yet in the war—marked the turning point of the Revolution. In Europe, the news shook Parliament and Lord North's war machine. It had a powerful impact in France as well. Now that Louis XVI and his advisers were convinced that the Revolution was more than a family squabble—and that America could field an army capable of beating the finest professional European troops, they were willing to join in a war against their old adversaries, the British. They had last fought Britain in the 1760s, during the French and Indian Wars, and here was a chance to gain back lost ground.

In February, France and the United States signed an alliance, and the Revolution became a world war.

On Bemis Heights, New York's Saratoga National Historical Park commands the narrowest passage along the Hudson River's west bank. By defeating the British here, the Americans brought France into the war and kept control of the Hudson. Saratoga marked the turning point of the war.

Ragtag Ruffians Face Off Against

The image of the smartly dressed Continental soldier—largely drawn from the end stages of the war, when there were fewer men to clothe and more French funds—belies the hard reality many men faced. In lean times, patriot soldiers often went barefoot, their clothes reduced to rags. Even during well-clothed times, there was little uniformity among American soldiers' uniforms.

In 1777, Washington ordered patriot soldiers to wear a sprig of evergreen in their hats. Convinced that proper outfits would bolster morale, he issued a uniform code in 1779. All soldiers should wear blue coats, with facing in different colors on collars, cuffs, and lapels: white for New Englanders, red for those from the middle states, and light blue with a white edge and buttonhole lace for the Carolina and Georgia regiments.

With uniforms in short supply, the hunting shirt became a standard article of clothing in camp and on the battlefield. Made of deer leather, homespun, or linen, the shirts were edged with fringe, to channel water from seams and keep the wearer dry. Washington noted that the hunting shirt caused "no small terror to the enemy," since it gave the appearance of the much-feared frontier marksman.

The British Army was organized into infantry companies and regiments, and uniforms suited the regiment. Many—not all—British soldiers wore scarlet uniforms faced in white, some designed as waistcoats and some tails, with pewter buttons. Officers' uniforms boasted elegant ornamentation, like sashes and epaulets. All British soldiers had special parade dress, often including white cross-belts and brass medallions.

British and patriot armies made use of light cavalry—lightweight men on fast horses. Their leather or brass helmets sported long horsehair crests, which looked gallant but also protected riders' heads and necks from the slash of a saber.

Redcoat Regalia

The bond of respect deepened
between Washington and
the soldiers he commanded.

Downcast soldiers huddle over a fire at Valley Forge, Pennsylvania. Though not especially snowy, the winter of 1777-78 was marked by terrible privation and suffering. With outbreaks of smallpox and typhus, and men going barefoot, as many as one in four became unfit for duty. "Had there fallen deep snows," wrote a private, "the whole army must inevitably have perished."

The Revolutionary War

Chapter Five

While Burgoyne was threatening the rebels from the north, Washington kept an anxious eye on Sir William Howe and his army in New York. As the spring of 1777 turned into summer, Howe remained hunkered down, refusing to take the field, yet still preventing Washington from sending any more than a few regiments (and Benedict Arnold in person) to help first Schuyler, then Gates contain Burgoyne. There was always a good chance, Washington reasoned, that Howe might take his army up the Hudson in support of Burgoyne if the Continental Army left its winter quarters at Morristown, New Jersey.

Actually, Howe had no intention of giving Burgoyne more than minimal support. He was fixated on avenging his defeats at Trenton and Princeton. He had received neither directives nor additional troops from London, so he made his own plans, intending to capture Philadelphia and, with the thousands of Tory volunteers he expected to find in Pennsylvania, deliver a knock-out blow to Washington's ill-equipped and half-trained Continentals.

By July 1777, Howe was ready to move—and it was his plan to move by sea. The Royal Navy's massive flotilla sailed out of New York Harbor on July 23. Washington did not dare move in any direction. He refused to be lured into a trap, but he had no idea where Howe was going. The British fleet was spotted in Delaware Bay on July 31, then it disappeared. Not until August 25 did Howe's design become clear, when his troops landed at what is now Elkton, Maryland, at the head of Chesapeake Bay. Washington realized that he had to march south and defend Philadelphia.

On September 9, 1777, Washington arrayed his army along Brandywine Creek, 20 miles west of Philadelphia, ready to defend against Howe's, on the march north from the head of the Chesapeake.

PRECEDING PAGES: *In winter camp at Valley Forge, Gen. George Washington reviews the troops who have not yet fallen to disease, starvation, and cold.*

Commanding the main American force were Nathanael Greene and "Mad" Anthony Wayne, a daring brigadier general from Pennsylvania. His nickname more likely referred to his passionate temper than to any tendency toward irrationality. Also fighting with Washington was a new major general, 19-year-old Marie-Joseph-Paul-Yves-Roch-Gilbert du Motier de La Fayette, a French marquis who would prove that along with deep pockets and a long name, he had a lion's heart. Lafayette soon became a close confidante of the commander in chief.

Two days later, on the morning of September 11, Howe decided to repeat the Long Island maneuver. Displaying in front, he sent troops around to the west to outflank the patriots. Attacked from two sides, the Americans just managed to stave off disaster, losing about 1,000 men to Howe's 500. Through several battles in early October, Washington took a beating, but the tenacious commander kept shifting, feinting, hitting, and never giving in.

On September 18—the day before the first battle at Saratoga—recognizing that the British were approaching, the Continental Congress decided to move from Philadelphia to York, Pennsylvania. One week later, Howe and his army entered Philadelphia in triumph. Most able-bodied men had fled the city, but women and children welcomed the British troops, along with a few loyalists, some from the local upper crust, and most of the city's Quakers, who rejected both war and revolution and looked to the British government for protection. Two weeks later, Washington attacked a British outpost that lay a few miles outside of Philadelphia, in Germantown. Howe repelled the attack, but he realized that the capture of the rebel capital city was inconsequential. He had failed to destroy Washington's army. Burgoyne's defeat at Saratoga remained the truly decisive military event of 1777.

While the British wintered in the warm and cheery houses of Philadelphia, the Continental Army huddled in lean-tos in the rolling farm country of Valley Forge, 20 miles north and west. The winter of 1777-78 was not especially cold—not nearly as bitter as two years later—though there was plenty of rain and mud. The real problem for the 10,000 soldiers at Valley Forge was supplies.

Congress, having no power to tax, could not raise money to feed and clothe its own Army properly, let alone pay its officers. From the beginning to the end of the war, American troops suffered from insufficient supplies. A shortage of tents left many soldiers exposed to cold winds and rain; the lack of clothes and blankets added insult to injury. Generals were constantly in need of guns, flints, artillery, bayonets, powder, and ammunition. General Gates once had his men tear up books for cartridge paper. While Congress tried to set up American gun and powder factories, forces in the field had to make do. Often the Army relied on captured supplies and on uniforms and arms sent by the French.

Deprivation marked the winter at Valley Forge, but greed is as much a part of the story as endurance. Farmers and merchants in Tory-leaning Chester County preferred selling their goods and products to the British. They would far rather receive payment in Britain's coin than in Congress's paper money, backed by nothing but promises. As a general rule, Washington forbade requisitioning, or seizing supplies from civilians, for he knew that to win the war he could not alienate the general population.

The Continental soldiers were forced to forage the countryside as far as they could, stripping it bare of firewood and food. Washington's troops languished for lack of medical gear, medicines, cooking equipment, bedding, uniforms, and, above all, food—they once went for six days straight with no meat. Given poor nutrition and substandard sanitation, sickness flourished. A quarter of the men who wintered at Valley Forge died there. Some men served their country simply by reporting for duty, getting sick, and dying.

FOLLOWING PAGES: Bare trees await spring at Valley Forge Historical Park, 20 miles from Philadelphia. In 1777-78, cold and hungry troops likewise waited for food and clothing. Because of a shoddy delivery system, supplies never arrived.

Revolutionary reenactors demonstrate drills taught by German-born Baron von Steuben, who joined Washington at Valley Forge as a military expert. By the end of the hard winter, the Prussian taskmaster had disciplined the rough-hewn American brigade into a well-oiled fighting machine.

For all its privations, Valley Forge proved a pivot point for the Continental Army. The men who endured together in that Pennsylvania countryside emerged six months later a tougher, more unified fighting unit than ever before. To begin with, an inept quartermaster general resigned in November, and Washington replaced him with the capable soldier, Nathanael Greene, who rolled up his sleeves and went to work on the problematic supply situation. Before the winter was over, thanks to Greene's efforts, Washington's soldiers were rolling in meat, flour, whiskey, clothes, guns, and ammunition. Providence pitched in with a good run of spring shad in the Delaware River. As the land greened and the air softened, the soldiers were reinvigorated. The bond of mutual respect deepened between the patrician Washington and the ordinary soldiers he commanded. New recruits poured in, and the head count grew to more than 13,000.

WHILE THE CONTINENTAL ARMY was surviving at Valley Forge, some in Congress were having second thoughts about keeping Washington in command. In comparison with Gates, who had just defeated Burgoyne in a big way, Washington looked a bit second-rate, constantly being pushed around by Howe. Congress had just been forced to flee

The Revolutionary War

J am well aware of the Toil and Blood and Treasure, that it will cost Us to maintain this Declaration, and support and defend these States. — Yet through all the Gloom I can see the Rays of ravishing Light and Glory.

JOHN ADAMS, IN A LETTER TO HIS WIFE, ABIGAIL ADAMS, JULY 3, 1776

Philadelphia and was perhaps feeling the need to assert itself. Several Northerners wanted to consider replacing Washington with Gates, or at least someone they could control better.

In a letter to Gates, an Irish-born French officer named Thomas Conway complained of Washington's incompetence. A series of back-and-forth accusations ended with Washington's handing over a batch of correspondence to the congressional Military Committee. Whether or not there was an actual plot afoot—probably there was none—Gates and Conway came out looking like lowly intriguers. Conway was forced to resign and left the country after apologizing to Washington. The affair died out as the war heated up in the summer of 1778, leaving Washington more esteemed than ever in patriot eyes.

But the chief blessing to the Continental Army at Valley Forge was an imposter from Germany. Calling himself Frederick William Augustus Henry Ferdinand, Baron von Steuben, he claimed to be a nobleman, owner of a huge estate, and to have served as lieutenant general under Frederick the Great, considered the reigning military genius of the time. In fact, he did serve in Frederick the Great's army in the Seven Years' War, but never as more than a captain. He was an adventurer, an original American type—here to seek fame if not fortune. Congress was impressed with him—and with his offer to serve for no pay until he had proved himself—and he was appointed adjutant general, an assistant to the commanding officer.

When von Steuben saw the ragged condition of the soldiers at Valley Forge, he realized they would have been a challenge for Frederick the Great himself. He started from scratch, training these raw recruits in the fundamentals, then drilling them until they could march in lockstep in their sleep. For all his posing, the hard-driving, hot-tempered Prussian did know what he was doing, and he set about it with a will. He spoke a little French and less English, but translators and body language made up for the deficiency. The soldiers quickly got used to Steuben's thundering "God damns!" They saw that he had a sense of humor, and they came to admire their taskmaster. At the same time, he had the wisdom to understand that he could not make perfect Prussian soldiers out of American farm boys. In a letter to a European friend, he wrote, "You say to your soldier, 'Do this,' and he does it. But I am obliged to say to my soldier, 'This is the reason why you ought to do this,' and *then* he does it."

Steuben trained the Continentals in the use of the bayonet. He taught them how to charge and retreat, and he compiled a manual of military drills that became standard thoughout the states. By the time troops left their winter camp, the Continental Army was forged into an organized, disciplined fighting unit, equal to the British. If the righteousness of their cause had kept them going before, they now were proud of their skills as well. A much more confident army took to the field in June.

Washington's old adversary, Sir William Howe, was by now bowing out. Shortly after his forces had occupied Philadelphia the previous September, Howe learned of Burgoyne's defeat at Saratoga. He used the news as leverage to depart a war that was wearying him, complaining as he did so that he had not been properly supported by London. Lord North accepted his resignation and replaced him with Sir Henry Clinton. Before Howe's May departure from Philadelphia, though, he was honored with an extraordinary send-off party by his officers and Philadelphia Tories, who arranged a Mischianza, or medley, of celebratory events, including a regatta on the Delaware River, a jousting tournament with officers dressed as knights vying for local girls in Turkish costumes, a feast, dancing, fireworks, and a midnight supper. Triumphal arches were raised for Howe and his brother, the admiral.

Shortly afterwards, the British Army got down to business. A wider war had broken out with France and Spain, meaning that Britain was engaged in several theaters: North America (the most prominent, and the only one Britain lost), but also the West Indies, Gibraltar, India, and home waters. Losing but one out of five wasn't bad from the British standpoint. Sugar interests in the Caribbean Islands were an ongoing concern, because French forces there continually tried to seize what they could. Clinton, having taken over command from Howe, received orders from London to send 5,000 men to the West Indies and to take the rest of his army back from Philadelphia to New York by sea.

He did neither. He lacked the fleet of ships available to the Howes in 1777—with the outbreak of war with France, the Royal Navy was needed elsewhere—so he marched his army overland the 70 miles from

Philadelphia to New York. By June 18, 1778, he and his roughly 11,000 troops were across the Delaware, ready to march. Dragging them down were 1,500 wagons of baggage and guns, the whole column several miles long. Clinton did send on to New York by ship some 3,000 loyalists who feared a patriot revenge.

Over in Valley Forge, Washington kept tabs on Clinton's movements across New Jersey and began to give chase. On June 26, Clinton's forces, heading toward Sandy Hook across the water from New York, staggered into Monmouth Courthouse, a small community in a swampy area of central New Jersey. It had been a stifling day for marching 19 miles through sandy soil in wool uniforms, carrying 60-pound packs. Many soldiers

Nathanael Greene

For his strategic brilliance in the final years of the war, Maj. Gen. Nathanael Greene ranks second only to George Washington among American commanders in the Revolution. Early on, he worked in his father's iron foundry, but by 1770 he had been elected to Rhode Island's General Assembly. He helped found a local militia, the Kentish Guards, but a stiff knee kept him from rising beyond the rank of private. His military career soon changed course, though: In 1776, having led troops to Boston, Greene was promoted to brigadier general in the Continental Army. Illness kept him from the Battle of Long Island, but he fought at Trenton, Brandywine, and Germantown. As quartermaster general at Valley Forge during the brutal months of early 1778, he showed his skill as an organizer. In 1780, fed up with congressional quibbles, Greene resigned. He soon returned to duty, though, when Washington asked him to command the southern army.

Greene never won a battle, but his dogged campaign staggered British efforts to gain a foothold in the South. In his biggest engagement—at Guilford Courthouse, North Carolina, in March 1781—he inflicted heavy losses on Cornwallis despite being driven from the field himself. "The battle was long, obstinate and bloody," Greene wrote. "Except the ground and the artillery, they have gained no advantage. On the contrary, they are little short of being ruined." After the war, Greene settled at Mulberry Grove, a Georgia plantation awarded to him by the state legislature for having driven the British out. A year later, at the age of 44, he died of sunstroke.

Washington to the rescue: In one of his finest moments at the Battle of Monmouth Courthouse, New Jersey, on June 28, 1778, George Washington rallied the troops and turned a disorderly retreat into a fierce attack and an American victory. In Emanuel Leutze's dramatic 1854 rendering of the action, Gen. Charles Lee slumps on his white charger, chastised for leading the retreat. It was to be Lee's last battle.

actually collapsed and died of heatstroke. But the next day they fanned out in position to face the Americans who had been nipping at their heels. The pursuers of two years ago in New Jersey were now the pursued.

Washington decided to hit—not with full force, but with more of a probing strike. He sent militia out to harry Clinton's wings on the morning of June 28, another day of oppressive heat and humidity. Up the middle he sent Gen. Charles Lee with 4,000 men. A veteran of the fight in 1776, Lee was an eccentric, hard-drinking, controversial officer with many years' experience on European battlefields. Earlier in the Revolution he was considered by some, including himself, a likely candidate for commander in chief, but he was turned down, partly

The Revolutionary War

because he was British-born and partly because he was not fully trusted. Though he had readily taken up the cause of independence, he had spent a year as Howe's prisoner, and during that time, he may have become convinced that America would do best within the British Empire—or he may have been pulling off an elaborate deception on the British: Historians are still not sure. What is clear is that at the time of his return from captivity, George Washington still trusted Lee.

But instead of working out a plan, Lee waited for things to develop in front of him. Finally he attacked, but found himself facing the main force of the British Army instead of the small rear guard he had been expecting. In the confusion of withdrawing across three ravines to

occupy a better position, his men and officers had no idea what was going on, and Lee was doing a poor job communicating his intentions. Washington came forward and saw what looked like a general retreat. The two generals yelled at each other—no one knows exactly what they said, but Washington showed himself a master of profanity. Lee was sent to the rear, and Washington rallied the troops to the offensive.

Lt. Thomas Lamb gave these silver spurs to his commanding officer, George Washington, as a memento of the pivotal winter of 1777-78 in Valley Forge, Pennsylvania, when he and 10,000 other soldiers survived and rose triumphant under Washington's command.

Three brigades attacked, led by distinguished officers: Nathanael Greene, "Mad" Anthony Wayne, and the Marquis de Lafayette, the young and able aristocrat who had arrived at his own expense from France and volunteered for the patriot cause. The Americans gave as good as they got, returning volley for volley at close range, withstanding charge after charge as never before. Washington and von Steuben watched proudly, the latter cursing gleefully in various languages. By evening the British fell back, exhausted, and in the morning they were gone, retreating to Sandy Hook, where they could cross to New York City.

Tactically, the engagement was a draw. Both sides suffered about 400 casualties, but the British withdrawal meant that the Battle of Monmouth Courthouse was considered their defeat by military convention. A more decisive patriot victory might have meant the end of the war.

The patriots did make some gains: The British lost 600 deserters, and Washington could wash his hands of Lee. The irascible General Lee wrote an angry letter to Washington, demanding a chance to defend himself. Washington ordered a court-martial. Lee was cleared of the charge of disobeying orders, but was temporarily dismissed from the Army. Haughtily, he responded by resigning. His later behavior suggested mental instability—he never stopped writing offensive letters, attacking Washington extravagantly. Congress paid him no heed, and he died in poverty in Philadelphia less than five years later.

FOLLOWING PAGES: In July 1778, patriots defended Pennsylvania's frontier against an army of Iroquois and loyalists. Outnumbered 900 to 360, they met a crushing defeat in the Wyoming Valley. The enemy destroyed 1,000 homes, took 227 scalps, and spread fear throughout the region.

Only a couple of weeks after the Battle of Monmouth Courthouse, Washington had a chance to strike a decisive blow against Clinton in New York, with the help of his newly arrived ally, the French fleet under the Comte d'Estaing. The 16-ship French armada had taken 87 days to sail from Europe, and then the ships could not make it across a sandbar at the mouth of Raritan Bay, behind Sandy Hook, where the Royal Navy squadron was anchored. D'Estaing decided to send 12 of his main battleships north instead, to capture Newport, Rhode Island. He might

The Revolutionary War

have succeeded, but for a storm and the prompt arrival of Admiral Lord Howe's smaller but formidable fleet. A few single-ship shoot-outs ended in a stalemate, and Newport remained in British hands. Eventually d'Estaing sailed south with his fleet, to defend the Caribbean island of Martinique against the British. Washington had to wait for another time to gain any benefit from this powerful ally. The French, after all, had their own agenda in this war, and helping the Americans was useful only insofar as it helped them beat the British.

MEANWHILE, THE WESTERN FRONT was becoming an ongoing theater with its own personality. To examine the roots of revolution in the West, we have to go back to the British Parliament's Royal Proclamation of 1763, which prohibited white settlement beyond the Appalachian Mountains. The decree was ostensibly established to prevent wars between Indians and settlers, thus protecting British outposts and avoiding the cost of building additional garrisons all through the Ohio

Her husband wounded, Mary Hays, below, took his place in an artillery crew at the Battle of Monmouth in 1778. Earlier on that sweltering June day, she had carried water to the men in battle. Hays is said to have smoked, drunk, and cursed like a regular soldier, but it was her bravery that earned her the nickname Molly Pitcher—a name used for several women who aided the American cause.

River Valley. But colonists looking for good land at a low cost—and those, like George Washington, eager to sell the real estate they had already staked out beyond the mountains—did not appreciate the proclamation. Nor did they heed it.

During the next decade, settlers kept trickling through the mountain gaps, setting up homesteads and communities in the vast territory between the Appalachians and the Mississippi. The lands south of the Ohio River were especially attractive—they were mostly neutral hunting grounds shared by the Cherokee, Shawnee, and others, unlike the territory controlled by the indomitable Iroquois Confederacy to the north. So while colonists in the East were worrying about British taxes, settlers were pushing into what is now Kentucky and Tennessee, and the British government was powerless to stop them. When it finally came to war, many of these tough, independent-minded backwoodsmen were more than willing to cross back over the mountains to help their fellow Americans achieve freedom.

In general, if Native Americans took sides at all, they chose to fight on the side of the British. After all, the crown had promised to keep settlers out of their lands, and as the war dragged on, such promises kept coming. In the thinly settled frontiers between the Great Lakes and the Gulf of Mexico, there were literally hundreds of armed clashes between Indians and whites. Often involving only a few hundred fighters, these wilderness battles, which were fought outside the rules of civilized warfare, were among the most brutal struggles of the entire Revolution. Indian villages and farms were routinely destroyed, prisoners tortured and killed, with little distinction made between combatants and noncombatants.

The blood flowed especially freely and steadily between the Mohawk Valley of western New York and the Wyoming Valley in northern Pennsylvania. American settlers thought that after the Saratoga victory, the area might enjoy some peace. It was not long before they discovered how wrong they were.

On July 1, 1778, a force of about 1,000 Tories and Iroquois swept down from Fort Niagara to the Wyoming Valley. Of the Six Nations of the Iroquois, only two—the Oneida and the Tuscarora—did not side with the British against the patriots. The others—the Mohawk, Cayuga, Onondaga, and Seneca—were determined to stop any further white advancement into their shrinking territory. So it was with a vengeful purpose that these American Indians descended upon the Wyoming Valley. Of the 300 frontier militia who opposed the Tory-Indian force, about 60 got away. The others were killed and scalped or captured and tortured to death. Defenders of two forts surrendered on the condition that homes would be spared. The promise was broken—cabins and mills were torched, stock was driven off, and survivors fled for their lives.

The Wyoming Massacre touched off a series of bloodbaths along the Mohawk and Cherry Valleys to the north. Families and neighbors

War in the outlands: Journeying down the Ohio from Pittsburgh to the Illinois country in the winter from 1778 to 1779, an invasion force under Lt. Col. George Rogers Clark dislodged the British from strongholds along the Wabash and Mississippi Rivers.

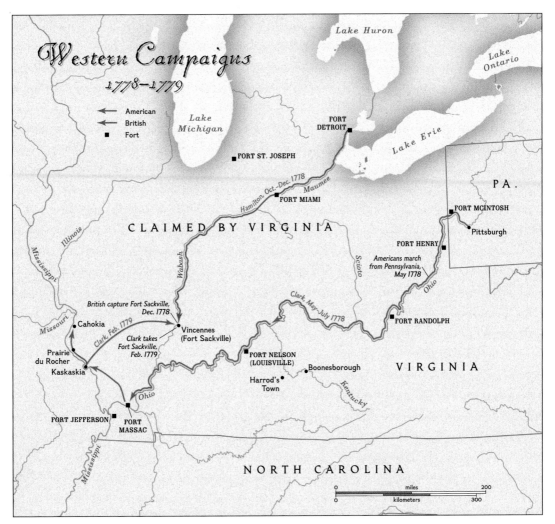

warred against each other. The Tory-Indian alliance had the upper hand until George Washington heard the news and decided to do something about it. It took a while for the American military to outfit a force for this farflung expedition, but by the summer of 1779, a contingent of several thousand Continentals was laying waste to the Iroquois country.

Following instructions, they scorched everything in their path—longhouses, orchards, gardens, and cornfields, all went up in smoke. They tried to capture and hold hostages, but most ran off to warn other villages. It was no use. The Continentals leveled 39 out of 40 Iroquois villages in central New York, in the process destroying a way of life the Indians would never fully reestablish. Barbarities occurred along the way—some dead Indians were scalped, and two were skinned by an officer, their flesh turned to hide to be used for leggings.

With British help, the Iroquois fought back until the war ended. They then retreated to Canada, their enmity with America bitter and lasting. A Seneca chief later said about Washington: "When your army entered the country of the Six Nations, we called you the town destroyer, and to this day, when that name is heard, our women look behind them and turn pale and our children cling close to the necks of their mothers."

FARTHER WEST, THE TERRITORY CALLED the Old Northwest, between the Ohio River and the Great Lakes, was a wild land of virgin forests and rich grasslands. It was ripe for the taking, and 26-year-old Indian fighter George Rogers Clark of Virginia—the older brother of William Clark, who together with Meriwether Lewis would later explore the West—thought he was the man for the job. The Virginia Assembly agreed. They commissioned him as lieutenant colonel and sent him out with 200 men to conquer a piece of land twice the size of Great Britain.

Clark's 1778 journey by land and water into the terrain that is now considered the American Midwest is an epic story of hardship and courage. His ultimate goal was to take Detroit, but first he had to confront the British, located in forts throughout the Illinois country. In February 1779 Lieutenant Colonel Clark marched his tired, hungry men 180 miles in 17 cold days to the outpost of Vincennes, on the Wabash River in today's Indiana. He immediately assailed the fort, held by less than a hundred men.

After his riflemen had picked off gunners at the portholes, he demanded the fort's surrender. To show he meant business, he ordered five captured Indians executed in full view of the fort. The Indian pawns in this grisly drama played their parts with bravery, singing their death song while one by one they were tomahawked. One chief, not dying at the first blow, removed the tomahawk and handed it back to his executioner. It took two more blows to kill him. Clark took the fort, but he never had sufficient manpower to move on to Detroit. His expedition did, however, help secure the Old Northwest.

In general the conflicts in the West were military dead ends. Spun off from the maelstrom back East, they caused damage but did not affect the overall course of the war. Ultimately, though, they established for the United States a strong claim to this territory during peace negotiations. And they set the stage for the decades ahead, when more and more settlers would displace Indians from their homelands.

AFTER FOUR LONG YEARS OF WAR, both sides were low on energy, money, and new strategies. The Revolution was not over, but neither side could figure out a way to bring it to a conclusion. So far, the South had seen a few small battles—but soon, the main theater of war would be shifting to that region.

A red sun rises over the midwestern terrain through which Lt. Col. George Rogers Clark traveled with his intrepid band in the winter of 1778-79. The 1,200-mile wilderness march gained for America the western frontier all the way to the Mississippi.

Women Create, Defend, and Care

for the New Nation

*B*efore a shot was fired, dedication to the cause of American liberty was demonstrated by the thousands of families that boycotted British manufactured goods in the 1760s and early 1770s. These boycotts would have been impossible without the support of women. Preparing homespun cloth rather than purchasing British wool and cotton, for example, required significant time, effort, and skill—and gave a vivid demonstration of a family's commitment to the patriot cause.

Women were the unsung heroes of the Revolutionary War: They either stayed at home and kept the shop or farm running or accompanied the troops and foraged, cooked, mended, and nursed. Several women served as spies, and at least one disguised herself to become a soldier. In 1782 Deborah Sampson, a Massachusetts substitute schoolteacher, cut her hair, bound her chest, and enlisted in the Fourth Massachusetts Regiment under the name Robert Shurtleff. She took a sword wound in the head and later a bullet in the shoulder, but a fever put her out of action. The doctor treating her discovered her secret, but he kept it to himself until she was honorably discharged and the war was over.

Abigail Adams, the wife of John Adams, was one of the truly notable women of the Revolution. She never occupied a public position, never made a speech or wrote a pamphlet. Like countless other wives, she endured long months—even years—of loneliness, while her husband was serving in Congress and as a diplomat abroad. Her correspondence with her husband reveals her as a tireless, observant writer. When he told her he was attending to the rights of man at Philadelphia, Abigail Adams pointedly asked her husband to "remember the ladies."

Martha Washington, above, mother of the country, appears full of purpose in a 1776 portrait. Opposite, an etching of a frontier woman reinforces Abigail Adams's admonition that "if perticular care and attention is not paid to the Ladies we are determined to foment a Rebelion."

Only in the South
could Britain hope
to make substantial gains.

to the South

A weather-beaten barn emerges from predawn darkness in the South, a region that attracted Britain's attention after three hard years of fighting farther north. With enough loyalist support, the British reasoned, it might be possible to save at least some of the colonies for the crown. They had not counted on fierce resistance from the southern backwoods.

Chapter Six

B y autumn of 1778, the war had stalled out in the North. The main British force was with Clinton in New York, the Continentals arrayed in the hills around them. The Americans could not push the British out, and the British could not subdue the Americans. After three and a half years, the war had stagnated into a series of inconsequential moves and countermoves. Lord North wanted to resign, but George III would not let him. It was His Majesty's opinion that Britain could still win the war—indeed, *must* win the war— for if she allowed America to break free, what message would that send to Britain's other colonies in the West Indies and elsewhere?

Despite what the King wished for, the British government had just about written America off—or at least part of it. Parliament was convinced by now that New England was gone, and probably all the North was gone, too. Many members of Parliament were adopting the attitude that letting go of the more obstreperous colonies might not be such a bad thing. If Georgia and the Carolinas could be reclaimed for the British Empire, it might help to regain Virginia. That would provide Britain a seaboard from the Chesapeake Bay down to Florida, plus Canada, and perhaps even a regained Northwest—still a significant British presence in America. Britain could also most likely hold New York City, Long Island, and adjacent regions, since they were strongly loyalist. So went the optimistic thinking of planners in London.

Part of this strategy hinged on the belief—which had proved wrong before—that Tory loyalists would come out in force to help the British regulars. Sir William Howe had warned that Tories would fight patriots only if British troops were backing them up, and that they could not hold an area once the British forces had moved on. But there was, in fact, reason to believe that Tories

PRECEDING PAGES: *Just beginning to fight, John Paul Jones's* Bonhomme Richard (right) *outduels the H.M.S.* Serapis *in the war's most dramatic sea battle.*

French and American troops gather outside Savannah, Georgia, in the autumn of 1779, preparing to lay siege to the port city that had fallen to the British the previous year. Despite a valiant effort, the allied campaign failed.

might be more supportive in the South. Plenty of Scotch-Irish farmers populated the Piedmont region of Virginia and North Carolina. Those farmers remained loyal to the crown, although many of them nursed old resentments against the upper class in Britain. It was also true that outspoken patriots were sparse among the genteel people of South Carolina and Georgia, who would support any government willing to guarantee their economic livelihood and their rights as plantation and slave owners.

Late in 1778, Clinton sent a force south: 3,500 Highlanders, Hessians, and loyalists, together with a Royal Navy squadron. On December 23 they dropped anchor off the coast of Georgia. To oppose them, a force of fewer than 1,000 patriots positioned themselves in the swamps outside Savannah. Executing a classic flanking maneuver, the British crumpled the American line and inflicted almost 500 casualties. By December 29, with only three dead and ten wounded soldiers, the British took over the port city of Savannah, along with all its ships, guns, and supplies.

Over the next few months, led by Gen. Augustine Prevost, who had

marched north from Florida with 2,000 troops, British forces solidified their hold on territory in Georgia. Prevost sent a column out to Augusta, 100 miles upland, following the Savannah River, and his forces easily captured that river port on January 29, 1779. Georgia's royal governor even returned from London, prepared to take back up responsibility for running the colony.

NEXT THE BRITISH MOVED into South Carolina. Prevost eyed Charleston, 70 miles up the coast from Savannah. By capturing it, the British would gain control over the three most important cities in Georgia and South Carolina.

During the British sweep through Georgia, patriots nearby had not been sitting idle. The whole southern countryside was beginning to erupt in ugly violence. Hundreds of loyalists joined up with the British, while small bands of patriot partisans made guerrilla hits against them. A long, vicious struggle was underway, similar to the conflict between Indians and whites on the northern frontier, with fights that would rack up scores still to be settled long after the war had ended.

FOLLOWING PAGES: Sunset gilds tidal flats of Ossabaw Island south of Savannah. On Christmas Day, 1778, British scouts pumped city residents for information. Four days later, British troops had reclaimed the key port from the Americans.

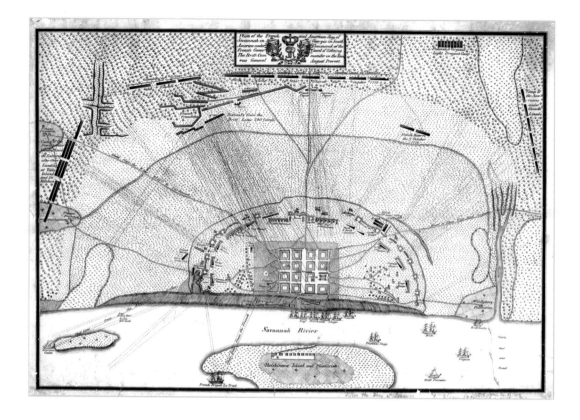

A map of Savannah shows the port town and its orderly squares surrounded by marshes—and, in September 1779, by French and American troops. British forces withstood the allied siege that took place on October 9, and the town remained under British rule for the rest of the war.

After the fall of Augusta, 700 North Carolina loyalists traveled south to join with the British in Georgia. They were checked at Kettle Creek, above Augusta, by the formidable Col. Andrew Pickens and his Georgia and South Carolina militiamen. Pickens, originally from Pennsylvania, had settled in South Carolina at the age of 24. He became one of the most famous Southern raiders, rising to brigadier general during the war. He later held office as a United States congressman. He soundly trounced the loyalists, only half of whom ever made it to Augusta. Five of the captured were later hanged as Tory ringleaders. The atrocities committed by both sides were appalling; even neutrals could not feel safe.

With 4,000 patriots, Gen. Benjamin Lincoln—a Northerner of large girth and small talents—hastened to Augusta, but he was pushed back from the city by combined British-Tory defenses. Lincoln had to retreat to Charleston, where Prevost and 3,000 troops were demanding the city's surrender.

Three years earlier, the patriots had held Charleston against a strong Tory attack. British warships had tried to bombard Fort Sullivan in June 1776, but the soft, spongy palmetto logs out of which it was

The Revolutionary War

constructed simply absorbed the cannonballs, and the British finally retreated. In commemoration of the battle, the fort was renamed for its commander, Col. William Moultrie. The South Carolina flag still sports an image of the protective palmetto.

Now, in May 1779, with the arrival of Lincoln's superior force, Prevost withdrew to Savannah, taking with him some 3,000 slaves, attracted by the promise of wider freedom, much to the consternation of their owners. In the long run, many of them were sold back into slavery in Britain's Caribbean colonies.

THE LANGUOROUS SUMMER HEAT BROUGHT HOSTILITIES to a pause in North America. But that September, related action took place across the sea.

Scottish-born John Paul Jones had come to the American colony of Virginia by way of the Caribbean. From 1775 on, commissioned by the Continental Congress, Jones waged sea battles on behalf of the patriot cause. In September 1779, he was sailing an old frigate loaned to him by the French king. Its name, *Bonhomme Richard*, was simply a French version of "Poor Richard," the fictitious character central to Benjamin Franklin's famous *Almanack*. Jones's mission was to keep the British commercial fleet in check by threatening any privateering moves in Atlantic waters.

On the evening of September 23, 1779, off the coast of Yorkshire near the town of Flamborough, Jones faced off with Britain's brand-new frigate, the H.M.S. *Serapis*, in the North Sea. The two ships commenced firing at each other. The *Bonhomme Richard* spouted so many holes that Jones's only hope for continued engagement was to throw out grappling hooks and

Father of the American Navy, John Paul Jones bedeviled British commercial ships throughout the war. His shining moment came during the September 1779 battle off the British coast. After the war he served as rear admiral in a Russian fleet.

board the *Serapis*. As he approached, the captain of the *Serapis* asked if Jones intended to surrender.

"I have not yet begun to fight!" Jones shouted back. With the two ships lashed together, the battle became a frenzy of muskets and grenades. Spectators watched from the shore as the ships caught fire and the sailors tried furiously to douse the flames. The locked ships pitched and twisted at anchor in the moonlight. The fighting raged on for two hours. Finally the British captain struck his colors. He

The Revolutionary War

To no avail, British frigates had fired on Fort Sullivan in Charleston Harbor earlier in the war, in June 1776. The fort's soft palmetto logs and sand absorbed the impact of cannon balls, and accurate American artillerists repulsed the attack, forcing three British ships aground.

handed over his sword and his ship. Jones took command of the *Serapis* and let the mangled *Bonhomme Richard* sink.

America now had a new naval hero to celebrate.

IN THE FALL OF 1779, the French Navy reentered the picture. On September 8, the Comte d'Estaing, the French admiral, sailed back from the West Indies in another bid to inflict harm on the British. Washington wanted him to come to New York City, but d'Estaing chose instead to focus on the South. So with 33 ships, 2,000 guns, and 4,000 troops, the French were back in force. Seeing their allies coming to their aid, patriot hearts lifted.

An old war aphorism maintains that the only thing worse than fighting with no allies is fighting with them. When d'Estaing demanded the surrender of Savannah "to the French," the Americans were none too pleased. Lincoln and the 1,300 troops he was leading from Charleston had not yet arrived, but when they did they were treated with arrogance by the French. William Moultrie—the Charleston native so important to the 1776 defense of that city, now a general—wanted to stage an assault, an all-out attack. D'Estaing said no, they should dig in for a siege—a surround-and-bombard campaign to cut off the town's lifelines and force it to surrender.

Two weeks later, impending hurricanes and the British fleet's approach forced him to change his mind, and d'Estaing decided to go for an assault after all. By now, though, the British had had time to prepare, girdling the town with earth and log entrenchments. Most of the 3,200 defending troops were American loyalists, a sign of the bitter civil-war dimension of the southern campaign.

On October 9, 1779, the French and Americans attacked the British at Spring Hill, just outside Savannah. With the French on the right, Americans on the left, five columns ran in sequence across 500 yards of open ground. They threw themselves against Prevost's defenses. The defenders gunned them down like sheep in a field. A few made it to the Spring Hill redoubt, including South Carolina militia under Francis Marion, the legendary local raider also called the "Swamp Fox."

For an hour, musket butts and bayonets churned up gore in the entrenchments. Cavalry units led by Casimir Pulaski—a Polish nobleman who had been recruited in France, had served at Brandywine, and had been commissioned by Congress to form an independent cavalry unit—tried to find a breach in the defenses. The cries of horses added to the uproar. Pulaski was mortally wounded, and his cavalry fell back.

Little by little, the attack was repulsed. The allies suffered almost 1,000 casualties, two-thirds of them French. British and loyalist losses totaled only about 150.

The failure to retake Savannah crushed American hopes. Southern patriots began deserting in droves, finding ways to make their own peace with the British. After failures in New York, Newport, and now Savannah, the alliance between America and France seemed on shaky ground. The British and American loyalists fighting with them were cementing a hold on the South, and they began casting their eyes with renewed interest on points north.

MEANWHILE, UP IN NEW YORK'S HUDSON VALLEY, Clinton was taking jabs at Washington, trying to entice him into a broad battle. To block the British from moving up the Hudson, Washington ordered the building of a major fortress at West Point, about 50 miles north of New York City. The new West Point fortifications were designed and built by Pulaski's fellow Pole, Thaddeus Kosciuszko, a military engineer whose breastworks had helped Gates win the Battle of Saratoga. Ten miles south were two smaller forts. They helped protect West Point, and Clinton decided to harass Washington by seizing them. The British thereby gained the strategic position of Stony Point, a high, rocky promontory overlooking the Hudson River. They installed 600 troops there, mostly loyalists.

Washington had surveyed Stony Point carefully during the fort's construction, and he believed it could be recaptured by a surprise attack. He chose the intrepid "Mad" Anthony Wayne to carry out a daring midnight assault.

On the night of July 15, 1779, Wayne led 1,350 men south from West Point. It was to be a bayonet attack—they marched in silence with unloaded muskets, except for a few soldiers whose movements were meant to create a diversion. After wading across a marsh, up to their necks in water, Wayne's troops stormed the fort.

The fighting was furious for several minutes. Wayne suffered a slight wound to the head, but his troops quickly overwhelmed the British, who threw down their weapons. Even in the dark, Wayne's men showed great restaint, and the killing, which

In 1780 Britain pinned its dreams of Southern conquest on 42-year-old Charles, Earl Cornwallis. Not content simply to hold Georgia and South Carolina, the aggressive general struck boldly out for North Carolina and Virginia. The gamble would cost him his entire army in 1781 at the climactic siege of Yorktown.

often got out of hand in the close confines of a fort, was rapidly brought to a halt. With less than one hundred casualties, Wayne and his forces were able to capture the whole garrison brilliantly.

Washington followed up this success with another small victory a month later, led by "Light-Horse Harry" Lee. A dashing cavalry commander, Lee was destined to become governor of Virginia, the father of Robert E. Lee, and the author of the memorable eulogy of George Washington as "first in war, first in peace, and first in the hearts of his countrymen."

Lee succeeded in capturing a British post at Paulus Hook, New

Jersey—today, part of Jersey City—in that summer of 1779. Thanks to that victory and a few other morale boosters, General Washington took his Continental Army into winter quarters, hopeful that the next year would bring him, his men, and his country more propitious circumstances.

First, though, his fatigued soldiers had to endure yet another trial. The winter of 1779-80 at Morristown, in upper New Jersey, was the worst of the entire war.

Washington's 10,000 men stripped the surrounding hills of all possible wood, but the fires they built did not keep them warm. Many soldiers sickened and died; others deserted. Amid the hardships, unleavened by any hope of proper remuneration, it was no wonder that mutinies broke out. After short rations for weeks, unpaid for five months, two Connecticut regiments started to march home. A Pennsylvania regiment halted them. Ordinarily, stiff punishments would have been meted out for desertion, but Washington responded leniently, which made the whole issue recede into the background, as the troops prepared for yet another season of war.

In 1780 redcoats dug in, preparing to besiege Charleston. After 45 days of bombardment—"as if the stars were tumbling down," wrote an American officer— the city and its 5,500 patriot defenders gave up.

REALIZING THAT ONLY IN THE SOUTH could Britain hope to make any substantial gains, Clinton sailed out of New York by the end of 1779. With him sailed Lord Cornwallis, second in command, and 8,000 troops. After a rough sea voyage, they landed at Savannah and marched toward Charleston. Having failed to take that key port the previous year, the British now were determined to do so. Proceeding up the coast, they began to realize that Charleston was not going to give up without a fight. Clinton sent to New York for reinforcements. By April 1780, with 10,000 men, Clinton had laid siege on Charleston.

The British belt cinched tighter and tighter around the city, cutting off escape routes to the east, the south, and the west. General Lincoln considered his tenuous position, inside Charleston with 5,500 patriot troops. He could still escape and save most of his force, but city and state officials wanted him to stay and defend the city. Heeding their wishes was a grave error.

The British lines were edging in ever closer. Under steady bombardment, buildings were going up in flames. Then a young

Francis Marion

Most able of the South Carolina raiders, the legendary patriot Francis Marion was well into his 40s when Charleston fell into British hands. A war-related injury was said to have rendered him unfit for service, but he organized a team of hit-and-run guerrillas that antagonized the enemy through the rest of the war.

Raised near Georgetown, South Carolina, Marion knew the swamps like the back of his weathered hands. Whether staging lightning strikes on British outposts or scouting out enemy movements, Marion kept the patriot cause alive when the Carolinas appeared lost. British commander Cornwallis was so harassed by Marion that he sent his notorious cavalry leader, Banastre Tarleton, to hunt him down. "The devil himself could not catch the damned old fox," Tarleton later exclaimed.

From a base on Snow's Island in the Pee Dee River near Johnsonville, the Swamp Fox worked effectively with Nathanael Greene in his 1781 campaign, skirmishing and cutting off enemy supply lines. In the battle at Eutaw Springs, northwest of Charleston, he commanded the North and South Carolina militias as well as his own brigade.

A natural leader with a particular genius for guerrilla tactics, Marion was kind, brave, introverted, and semiliterate. His personal code of honor could seem contradictory—he would ignore truce flags and shoot enemy pickets, yet also forgive Tories and court-martial compatriots. After the war, he served in the South Carolina Senate.

British lieutenant colonel named Banastre Tarleton led a successful attack on a cavalry unit that was protecting the only avenue of patriot escape, north of the city.

The British capture of Charleston was complete. On May 8, Lincoln offered to surrender, as long as his forces could parade with the honors of war and his militiamen could return home. Clinton refused these conditions and began a massive artillery barrage. Four days later, Lincoln capitulated. He and his entire army were taken prisoners. The militia was later allowed to go home on parole.

When Charleston fell into British hands in 1780, many capable leaders were captured. Others slipped away and continued heckling the British. The "Swamp Fox," Francis Marion; the "Gamecock," Thomas Sumter; and Andrew Pickens organized teams of hit-and-run raiders that continued to antagonize the enemy through the end of the war.

Sometimes their operations would erupt into full battles. At other times, a few loyalist or British marks would end up swinging with the Spanish moss or lying in the moonlit swamps. Whether in pitched battle or in a lightning strike, these guerrillas kept the patriot cause alive when the South appeared lost. Because of such partisans, more battles were fought in South Carolina than in any other state during the Revolution. Sumter, for whom Fort Sumter in Charleston Harbor was named, went on to serve as a United States senator. He lived until 1832 when, at the age of 98, he was the last surviving general of the American Revolution.

THE FALL OF CHARLESTON WAS THE WORST patriot defeat of the war. To save themselves and their property, numerous gentlemen of the South Carolina squirearchy pledged loyalty to the crown. One, for example, was Henry Middleton, a former president of the Continental Congress and father of Arthur Middleton, who had signed the Declaration of Independence. The Middleton family ranked among the three or four most prestigious and wealthy of the South. Although they were able to hold onto their property, having to kowtow to the British was a blow to their pride. Over the long run, such a blow was equalled in humiliation only by the burning of the Middleton mansion by Union Gen. William Tecumseh Sherman's troops, which occurred nearly a century later during the Civil War.

Clinton departed for New York, leaving Cornwallis with instructions to take a defensive posture and then, if prudent, to advance northward. "I leave Lord Cornwallis here in sufficient force to keep it against the world, without a superior fleet shews itself," he wrote prophetically, "in which case I despair of ever seeing peace restored to this miserable country." He knew that the prospect of British victories had a way of disappearing once the battle was on. Those Americans kept rising again like so many phoenixes. That superior fleet would eventually arrive, though not in Charleston.

Nathanael Greene took command of the Southern Department from Horatio Gates, at right, after the latter's disastrous defeat at Camden in 1780. Greene won the campaign by keeping the British penned in port towns. Cornwallis considered him "as dangerous as Washington."

The high-energy Cornwallis was not one to sit back and do nothing. When a group of 350 Continentals arrived outside Charleston, too late to help with its defense, Cornwallis unleashed Tarleton, the vain and audacious new British star.

Tarleton chased them back nearly to the North Carolina border. He led a force of loyalists, largely from New York, into brutal battles of Americans against Americans. Tarleton's forces attacked and killed the Continentals mercilessly, continuing even after their adversaries had waved the white flag. More than 100 Continentals died, and most of the 200 taken prisoner were badly wounded. Tarleton earned a hateful reputation among low-country patriots, and he took on the nickname "Bloody Tarleton." Indeed, by sending Tarleton off after the Americans, Cornwallis had done nothing but stir up a hornet's nest of resistance.

Word began circulating that Congress was preparing to make a peace deal with the British, granting them Georgia and South Carolina. To put those rumors to rest, Congress resolved in June that "this Confederacy is most sacredly pledged to support the liberty and independence of every one of its members." In response to the Southern problem, Congress dispatched Horatio Gates. He dutifully marched South, accompanied by 1,300 men, whom he ostentatiously called his "grand army."

Bogged down in the bug-infested pine scrubs of North Carolina, Gates made slow progress. He augmented his army with militia until it numbered about 4,000. Hot, tired, and hungry, they trudged through the Carolina backcountry, meeting Tory sympathizers at every turn. They ate what they could find—green corn, unripe fruit, and half-cooked meat—until many fell ill with dysentery. Cornwallis, meanwhile, set out with about 2,500 troops to intercept Gates. Just north of Camden, South Carolina, on August 16, 1780, the two forces collided.

Cornwallis struck first, targeting the American left wing with a fearsome bayonet charge. The Virginia militiamen posted there had never faced an enemy before. They buckled immediately and took off running. The North Carolina militia, in the center, picked up on the pandemonium and likewise caved in. The Continentals moved up into the vacuum and tried to hold back the British onslaught, but their enemy smelled fear and closed in for the kill.

Finally, with so many redcoats swarming the field, the whole American line collapsed. They tore north, Tarleton hot on their heels. The Americans suffered 600 casualties, the British half as many, and, just as bad, the tactical loss brought humiliation to the patriots. To top it off, two days later Tarleton caught up with a patriot detachment led by Thomas Sumter, one of the famous South Carolina raiders. After killing 150 and capturing over 300, Tarleton's forces dealt the Americans a decisive defeat.

ONE MIGHT WELL ASK WHAT HAPPENED TO HORATIO GATES, the victor of the Battle of Saratoga, during the South Carolina debacle. If Gates had staged a more orderly retreat, he might have salvaged part of the day, but instead he fled to Charlotte, 60 miles north, then dashed another 120 miles to the northeast, to Hillsboro, North Carolina— all in three days, compared to the two weeks it had taken his army to cover less ground as they were heading south. This venture ended his career in the Continental Army. The kindest summation of his military service is that he made a better administrator than he made a soldier.

Gates was out. Cornwallis was the new hero of the hour. His stock soared among southern loyalists and among war planners and observers in England as well. Perhaps, the British surmised, in Cornwallis they had finally found a man who could beat Washington and douse the flames of revolution in America once and for all.

As for Washington, the loss at Camden meant he could replace Gates with his own choice for commander. Washington chose Nathanael Greene, already his right arm, destined to come through a hero of the Revolution without ever winning a battle. Greene's dogged persistence, amounting to brilliance, was soon to absorb and confound the British in the South.

Cypresses along a sinkhole in Francis Marion National Forest reflect the kind of soupy refuge that sheltered the "Swamp Fox" and other South Carolina raiders.

Three Heroes, Two Spies, and

Any soldier caught behind enemy lines without wearing a uniform was assumed to be a spy and subject to immediate execution.

For example: A few days after New York fell to William Howe's army in September 1776, the city went up in flames. Tories were thick on Long Island, and they suspected that patriot arsonists set the blaze. They arrested a young man, a recent Yale graduate, who had talked too much, making little effort to conceal the fact that he was gathering information for Washington's army. Little wonder that, on September 22, he was summarily hanged as a spy. On the gallows, young Nathan Hale uttered those famous words, "I only regret that I have but one life to lose for my country."

On the other hand, Benedict Arnold took nearly three years to go from glory to shame. His dramatic leadership on the field at Saratoga had been vital to the crucial American victory. Had he died there, he would be remembered, like Hale, as one of America's great heroes. But in the summer of 1778 Arnold went to Philadelphia as military governor of the city. Living far beyond his means, the 38-year-old major general began speculating in business, sometimes of a questionable character.

Arnold rubbed shoulders with loyalists as well as patriots. He was court-martialed on various charges, some trumped up. Feeling unappreciated and cash-strapped, he began working his Tory connections. For 16 months, until he was discovered, Arnold supplied valuable information to the British, primarily through General Clinton's aide-de-camp, John André. Appointed commander at West Point in the summer of 1780, Arnold schemed to deliver this key fortress, with Washington in it, to the British for £20,000—"a cheap purchase," he told Clinton.

On July 17, 1777, British commander William Howe wrote this letter to Gen. John Burgoyne, then en route to Saratoga, advising him of strategic plans. To keep it secret, Howe rolled up the paper strip tightly and tucked it into the hollow quill of a feather pen.

One Famous Traitor

Before the plan could be consummated, the plot was revealed. John André was captured, and Clinton refused to exchange him for the more treacherous Arnold. General Washington's hand shook as he signed the order for André's execution, which by the rules of warfare had to be carried out. All who witnessed the British soldier's hanging testified to his grace and bravery.

Meanwhile, Arnold stayed safely in the British fold. He led British troops, wreaked damage in Connecticut, and burned Richmond, Virginia, but he never gained the full trust of the British. After the surrender at Yorktown, Arnold urged George III to keep fighting, as though a British triumph could justify his treachery. He died, demoralized, in London in 1801.

Questioned by Americans, British Maj. John André reveals plans of West Point hidden in his boot. Soon André was discovered to have been working for Benedict Arnold, providing secrets to the British high command. Convicted of spying, André was hanged.

ng in possession of Ticonderoga, which is a great Event carried without Loss. I have rec. your two Letters Viz. fro in a double wooden Canteen, you will know if it was of any consequence; nothing of it has transpired to us. I will observe Ju to Albany — my Intention is for Pensilvania where I expect to meet Washington, but if it goes to the Northw. contrary to my

*The allied forces were coming
together like pieces on a chessboard,
with Cornwallis playing the part of
the king under attack.*

A lone forest grave in South Carolina's King's Mountain Military Park marks
the final resting place for Col. Patrick Ferguson, leader of a western wing of Cornwallis's army.
Fierce action here in October 1780 resulted in a landslide victory for patriot backwoodsmen.
Jefferson called the battle "that turn of the tide of success" that led straight to Yorktown.

The Revolutionary War

Chapter Seven

*F*lush with success after Camden in August 1780, Cornwallis struck out to the north. By late September he had taken up a position in Charlotte, North Carolina, a crossroads town and, he believed, a hotbed of patriot resistance. His plan was to sweep northward gradually, rallying loyalists along the way as he moved toward a final victory, at least in the South.

On his west flank, Cornwallis dispatched a 36-year-old colonel, Patrick Ferguson, a Scotsman whose method of conquering the hilly countryside was to issue a warning: If the settlers in the area—present-day western North Carolina and eastern Tennessee—did not quit their opposition to British arms, he would march an army in, hang the rebel leaders, and devastate the land. To the "over-mountain men" of the Southern Appalachians, this proclamation had an immediate effect—and not the one Ferguson hoped for. The independent-minded frontiersmen picked up their squirrel rifles and headed out in droves, intent on stopping Ferguson in his tracks.

On foot and on horseback, one group joined up with another, marching from the hills and hollows until they numbered about 1,400. They covered some 220 rugged miles in a mere two weeks. Hearing of the approaching opposition, Ferguson took his battalion of 1,100 loyalists east in search of better ground to make a stand. He found what he thought he was looking for at a Blue Ridge spur called King's Mountain, on South Carolina's northern border. When the patriots learned that Ferguson might be trying to elude them, they sent 900 of their best horsemen out in pursuit—a terrific sprint of 50 miles in 36 hours.

On October 7, 1780, the patriots encircled the base of King's Mountain and began to work their way up. Taking cover in a forest of tremendous oaks and poplars, they withstood one bayonet charge after another, picking off the loyalists with shots from their long rifles.

PRECEDING PAGES: At the 1781 surrender at Yorktown, patriot Gen. Benjamin Lincoln, victorious, receives British Gen. Charles O'Hara, on foot. Washington looks on.

In the thick of battle, Ferguson sat on his horse, giving orders with a piercing silver whistle and making an easy target of himself. Several bullets slammed into him and he slumped over dead, dragged along with a foot caught in the stirrup.

A cheer went up from the patriots as they swarmed about the loyalists, exposed in a meadow atop the mountain. Yelling "Tarleton's quarter," they showed that they intended vengeance for the havoc meted out by Tarleton's loyalist legion in Charleston. The enraged patriots kept on killing, even when survivors raised a white flag.

The Revolutionary War

It was one of the most complete victories of the war: Except for the few members of the company who missed the battle because they were out foraging, the loyalist force was totally wiped out, with 320 dead or wounded and 698 taken prisoner. The patriots suffered only 90 casualties. Marching the captives up to Hillsboro, the patriots paused long enough to hang nine of the Tory leaders.

At King's Mountain, British momentum in the South was severely checked. After General Cornwallis received the dispiriting news, he decamped back to South Carolina to think things over.

Now in charge of the ruins of the American Army left by Gates in South Carolina, Nathanael Greene split his small army of 2,000, sending Daniel Morgan and a force of 600 around to assail the British flank from the west. With so few men, Morgan could move quickly out of the way if things got too hot, Greene figured. When Cornwallis saw what Greene was up to, he could not believe his luck. He dispatched Tarleton with some 1,100 troops to take Morgan out of the picture.

One of the most capable commanders of the Revolution, Daniel Morgan had been a teamster—driving horse and mule teams that pulled wagons—during the French and Indian War. For defying a British officer, he had been sentenced to 500 lashes. He later said that the man assigned to flog him stopped at 499, so the British still owed him one. A decade later, he got his chance. Recruiting a company of Western

For a shining moment, cocky Colonel Ferguson and his loyalists had the momentum on King's Mountain in the Carolinas in October 1780. But patriot sharpshooters overwhelmed them from thick woods and surged to the top, taking the entire enemy force.

FOLLOWING PAGES: British troops, silhouetted at dawn, surrender their arms in a reenactment of the Battle of Cowpens, South Carolina, where Americans overran a superior British force on January 17, 1781.

Col. Tarleton is said to be on his way to pay you a visit.
I doubt not but he will have a decent reception
and a proper dismission.

NATHANAEL GREENE, IN A LETTER TO DANIEL MORGAN, 1781

riflemen at the outset of the Revolution, he had served with Arnold in Quebec. An ordinary man given the chance to become an extraordinary leader, Morgan's brilliance lay in understanding what his soldiers were capable of, then inspiring them to do it.

Like Arnold, Morgan had been passed over for promotion after his success in Quebec. But instead of turning coat, as Arnold did, Morgan just resigned. Now Congress needed him in the South and commissioned him as brigadier general. Collecting enough militia to nearly equal Tarleton's forces, he picked an open piece of ground known locally as "the Cowpens," not far west of King's Mountain. While awaiting the inevitable attack by the hotheaded Tarleton, Morgan laid out his plan, and on January 16, 1781, the night before the battle, he went over and over the details with his men.

He arrayed his forces in three lines—riflemen out front, then militia, and finally his Continentals on a slight rise. The first two lines were to get off two shots, preferably hits on officers, then they were free to retreat to safety, allowing the seasoned Continentals to absorb the bayonet charge, against which, Morgan knew, the militiamen could never be expected to stand. Behind a hill in the rear, Morgan concealed a body of cavalry.

As expected, Tarleton drove his troops directly into battle, intending to blow the Americans away with a frontal assault. The first two American lines did as they were ordered, making their shots count. Rebuffed but not stopped by the riderless horses that came streaming back, Tarleton pressed on, mistaking the planned militia flight for panic. The line of Continentals fell back, then, rallied by Morgan, got off a final volley and swept downhill in a bayonet charge.

Tarleton's line crumpled. He tried to regroup his cavalry, but it was too late—they had fled at the sight of Morgan's counter-attacking Continentals. The final damage was 100 British killed, 800 captured or wounded, versus 12 Americans dead and 60 wounded. The dreaded Tarleton had been toppled. The Battle of Cowpens was a resounding victory for Morgan and a stride forward for the American cause.

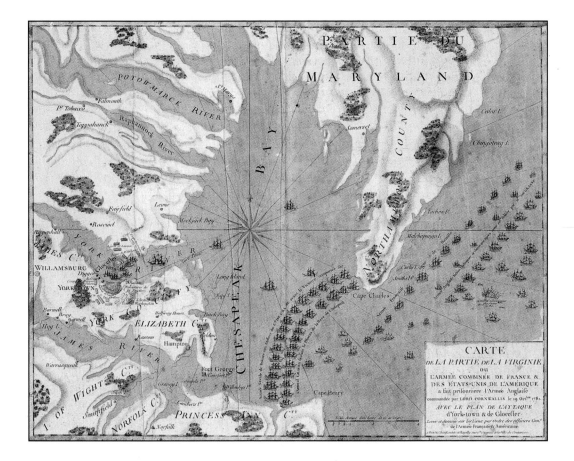

An 18th-century French map shows the battle lines around the Virginia capes in the fall of 1781. The French fleet blocked British ships from entering the Chesapeake Bay, allowing Washington and his ally, the French commander Comte de Rochambeau, to blast away at land forces led by British General Cornwallis in Yorktown.

Trying to make up for the loss, Cornwallis chased after Morgan. But the wily leader outpaced him, rejoining with Greene's army in central North Carolina. Finding himself pursued by Cornwallis, who was bristling for a battle, Greene wisely decided not to oblige until the odds looked better. He withdrew into Virginia, crossing the Dan River in boats designed to convert to wheeled carts for overland marches—vehicles he had prudently ordered when he reckoned the land ahead and its many streams. By the middle of March, Greene was back in North Carolina, installed at Guilford Courthouse, near present-day Greensboro—which was, in fact, named for Nathanael Greene. With his army now numbering more than 4,400, Greene was willing to do battle. Cornwallis had fewer than 2,000 able-bodied soldiers, but they were mostly top-drawer British regulars and Hessian professionals. Judging it a fair fight, Cornwallis decided to contest the field on March 15, 1781.

Greene decided to deploy in three lines, using the strategy that had worked for Morgan. Cornwallis struck the first line, composed of

French and British ships bombarded each other in a ferocious sea battle just outside the mouth of the Chesapeake. Though not a decisive victory, the French fleet bested the British in the September 1781 action. British Adm. Thomas Graves ordered his warships back to New York, leaving General Cornwallis without help, isolated in Yorktown. "We cannot succor him," Graves wrote at the time.

North Carolina militiamen. The militia fired, then peeled away, and the British pushed on to the second line, the Virginia militia. Taking several more hits, the British finally knocked heads with the steady-handed Maryland and Virginia Continentals of the third line. The fire-fight ended only when Cornwallis, desperate to win, ordered soldiers to fire grapeshot through their own ranks to push the Americans out—never mind the loss of his own men through intentional "friendly fire."

Greene pulled back, deciding that he had given and taken enough damage for one day. In doing so, he left the field—and the technical victory—to Cornwallis. But for a worthless piece of ground, Cornwallis had sacrificed more than a quarter of his force.

Greene's losses were smaller. Now slinking around each other like snarling dogs, Greene moved south and continued hounding the British, while Cornwallis took his battered, hungry army southeast to the port of Wilmington, North Carolina, explaining that he was "quite tired of marching about the country in search of adventure." More to the point, he desperately needed to resupply his troops.

MONTHS OF STEADY PRESSURE BY REBEL FORCES—both Greene's Continentals and local militiamen, waging guerrilla war in terrains they knew well—eventually loosened the British hold on everything in the South except the ports of Savannah, Charleston, and Wilmington.

Defying orders from Clinton, Cornwallis refused just to sit around defending Georgia and South Carolina. He still hoped to strike the devastating blow that would end this Revolution once and for all. Vaguely imagining that he could force some major issue in Virginia—which was as far north as his superiors had authorized him to go—he marched his men northward toward that erstwhile colony.

At Petersburg, Virginia, Cornwallis joined another British force, which included the turncoat Benedict Arnold. Now wearing a British uniform, Arnold advanced to Richmond, burning tobacco warehouses and destroying an American supply depot. In New York, Sir Henry Clinton simply threw up his hands. "My wonder at this move of Lord Cornwallis will never cease," he said. "But he has made it and we shall say no more, but make the best of it."

In fact, with 7,000 men or more under his command, Cornwallis wielded an impressive army. Washington, eager to catch and hang Arnold, had dispatched Lafayette with 1,200 Continentals to give the British something to worry about. Joined by Virginia militia and Wayne's Continentals, the little detachment of some 2,000 soldiers spent the early summer shadowing Cornwallis yet staying far enough away to avoid a major battle. But Cornwallis was determined to inflict as much damage as possible. The capture of Richmond forced the Virginia Assembly and Governor Thomas Jefferson to flee west. Cornwallis sent Tarleton raiding as far west as Charlottesville, his efforts to capture Jefferson and the legislature almost succeeding. Then Cornwallis turned his attention eastward. He marched his army to the end of the peninsula formed by the York and the James Rivers.

Clinton suggested to Cornwallis—but did not make it an order—that he establish a British base on the Chesapeake Bay. From there, he suggested that Cornwallis should send most of his troops north to New York, in preparation for a French naval assault there. Cornwallis decided to concentrate his men at Yorktown, a small settlement in southeastern Virginia, where the York River flows into the Chesapeake Bay. In early August 1781, Cornwallis set his men to fortifying that position.

MEANWHILE, WASHINGTON HAD LEARNED IN MAY that the French intended again to offer assistance. A potent fleet under the able command of Admiral François Joseph Paul, the Comte de Grasse, was en route to North America. In preparation for the fleet's arrival, Washington met in Connecticut with Jean-Baptiste-Donatien de

Redcoats bang the drums at a Yorktown reenactment. When the allied forces began their bombardment of the Virginia coastal town on October 9, 1781, Lord Cornwallis was shocked by the firepower. Unaware that the French had slipped siege guns past the British Navy, he was expecting only light shelling from field artillery. His headquarters was soon obliterated, and over the next few days, the bombing was incessant and deadly.

The Revolutionary War

Our venture in revolution and outlawry
Has justified itself in freedom's story
Right down to now in glory upon glory . . .

ROBERT FROST, "FOR JOHN F. KENNEDY HIS INAUGURATION," 1961

Vimeur, the Comte de Rochambeau, France's veteran naval commander. Their purpose was to discuss how to bring the war to an end. At first they considered capturing New York, where Clinton and his 10,000 troops were posted. But when it became clear that Cornwallis was amassing forces on the Chesapeake Bay, the French leadership urged Washington to switch gears. *Go for a large army rather than the large city,* they advised. Although Washington had been anxious to regain New York for a long time, he reluctantly saw the merits of the plan suggested by the French and agreed to it.

In August, Washington received confirmation that de Grasse was approaching the Chesapeake Bay with 28 French warships. The patriot general moved with alacrity, marching south to keep Cornwallis from escaping by land. The allied forces were coming together now like pieces on a chessboard, with Cornwallis not yet aware that he was playing the part of the king under attack.

Washington's Continental soldiers, augmented by Rochambeau's troops, began converging on Virginia. Simultaneously, the French squadron, under the Comte de Barras, set sail from Newport, Rhode Island, bound for the Chesapeake Bay. In early September, de Grasse debarked his 4,000 troops, so they could march by land and join Lafayette's forces outside Yorktown, Virginia, at the southern bight of the bay. The joint operation was coming off like clockwork.

At first, Clinton thought de Grasse would concentrate on New York. When he realized the danger approaching Cornwallis, it was too late. The trap had been set, and Cornwallis was boxed in. On September 5, 1781, Sir Thomas Graves arrived at the mouth of the Chesapeake, having led 19 British ships of the line from New York. De Grasse, already there, outmaneuvered Graves, inflicting damage on five of his ships. Graves's fleet retreated to New York for repairs. While those two forces had been engaged, de Barras had made his way into the Chesapeake. With 36 warships, the combined French fleet was now all but overwhelming. In the meantime, a juggernaut of

16,000 French and American troops, mostly well-equipped veterans supported by French money, was gathering around Yorktown.

Anxious about how all the elements would come together, Washington was overjoyed to find Cornwallis and the French fleet just where they were supposed to be. When Rochambeau arrived, he was amazed to see the dignified American commander jumping up and down, waving his hat, and grinning like a child. Cornwallis was in check. All that remained was to lay siege with such fierceness that he would cave in before Clinton could come to his rescue.

By the end of September, the American and French forces had drawn up and positioned themselves opposite the British

James Armistead Lafayette

At the time of the Revolution, some 20 percent of the American people—about 500,000 in all—were slaves. Such a vast labor pool did not go unexploited, used for political and military gain on both sides during the war. Five thousand black laborers, for example, worked for British General Cornwallis, who promised them their freedom after they built fortifications at Yorktown. In the midst of the siege, though, Cornwallis dismissed all the black workers suffering from smallpox. He hoped they would pass it on to his attackers.

A slave from Tidewater, Virginia, James Armistead received consent from his owner in 1781 to join General Lafayette's forces as they fought turncoat Benedict Arnold and his British troops. Pretending to be an escaped slave, Armistead infiltrated the British camps, posing as a guide and a servant. He supplied Cornwallis with false information about American troops and passed what he overheard among the British back to the Americans. Ultimately, Arnold sent him into Lafayette's camp, assuming his loyal service as a British spy.

Later, after surrendering at Yorktown, Gen. Cornwallis was surprised to see Armistead at Gen. Lafayette's headquarters, and to learn that he had been working for the Americans and the French, not for the British at all. After the war, Lafayette certified Armistead to be "entitled to every reward his situation could admit of." Granted his freedom in 1787, the ex-slave and dedicated patriot renamed himself James Armistead Lafayette.

Shortly after the British surrender at Yorktown, a Parisian engraver created this scene from verbal accounts. It shows de Grasse's massive fleet converging upon Yorktown—pictured here as a European city— while Cornwallis hands over his army to Washington and Rochambeau.

entrenchments. They busily set themselves to digging siege lines. From those trenches, encircling the enemy, the troops could blast away, slowly moving forward, digging new trenches, and tightening the circle.

On October 9, the bombardment began. It was a fearsome and nonstop barrage. With artillerymen firing an average of a shell a minute, the bombing continued 24 hours a day and lasted for nine days straight. A total of some 15,000 balls bashed the British fortifications, exploded overhead, and delivered an unceasing deluge of thunder, smoke, and menace. A British sally was easily beaten back, and a storm helped prevent a British escape by water.

On the night of October 14-15, 1781, bayonets in hand, the allies stormed two important redoubts. To ensure silence, Washington ordered his men to go in with unloaded guns. The French, planning to capture an adjacent redoubt, were allowed to load their guns but

expected not to shoot them. Both fortresses fell in less than 30 minutes, in one of the few instances of hand-to-hand action during the entire Yorktown campaign. The fall of Cornwallis's two fortresses meant that siege lines could move even closer. The allies could now bomb any spot in Yorktown they pleased with devastating accuracy. Half the town ended up destroyed in the process.

The siege had lasted another three days when a British drummer appeared on the ramparts, solemnly tapping out a request for a cease-fire. Up until then, Cornwallis had hoped a deus ex machina would appear in the form of Sir Henry Clinton and Sir Horatio Gates. "If you cannot relieve me very soon, you must be prepared to hear the worst," he had written to Clinton before the bombardment began.

Not until October 17 did Clinton set sail to the south, with a force of 7,000—but all in vain. With de Grasse's fleet blocking the bay, there was no way he could have reached Cornwallis—and, in any case, before he and his fleet had even made it that far, Cornwallis had surrendered. There was nothing to do but sail back to New York.

Cornwallis sent word to Washington that he was prepared to lay down arms, but only on the condition that his troops should be able to sail safely back to England. He pledged, in exchange, that they would not serve in the war anymore. But Washington demanded complete surrender. Lord Cornwallis, backed into a corner, had to submit.

On the afternoon of September 19, 1781, the British troops paraded through the allied ranks and laid down—or, in some cases, flung down—their weapons in a pile. The British and French soldiers were resplendent in their clean, neat uniforms. The American soldiers were a different lot. Washington and his staff came formally decked out, but the rank and file were a ragged bunch of hungry-eyed, battle-hardened soldiers, scruffy in appearance yet every inch proud victors.

Dejected, even tearful, the British behaved for the most part honorably, as did their captors. Cornwallis could not bring himself to attend the ceremony. Claiming he was indisposed, he sent Gen. Charles O'Hara to offer the sword of surrender. O'Hara ineptly tried to give the sword to Rochambeau, but someone discreetly motioned him to present it to Washington instead.

Observing strict protocol, Washington delegated a second to receive the sword. He chose General Lincoln, who had given up his own sword at Charleston a year and a half earlier. Lincoln symbolically took the sword from O'Hara, then handed it back to him. It is said that a British military band played "The World Turned Upside Down," a popular ballad. The words may have echoed through many redcoats' minds:

If buttercups buzz'd after the bee,
If boats were on land, churches on sea, . . .
If summer were spring and the other way round,
Then all the world would be upside down.

Having accepted Cornwallis's surrender, Washington dispatched a formal message to Congress: "I have the honor to inform Congress, that a reduction of the British Army under the Command of Lord Cornwallis, is most happily effected." Cornwallis and Clinton soon took leave of America, each blaming the other for the defeat. Clinton never recovered his reputation. He spent the rest of his life writing a history of the war, *The American Rebellion,* but it was never published until 20th-century scholars began to find it of interest. Cornwallis fared better, going on to serve in India, where he managed the British administrative system and quelled a local rebellion. He died in Ghazipore, India, and the Indian government still tends his grave.

With the surrender of more than 8,000 British soldiers and seamen, the 1781 Battle of Yorktown represented the climax of the Revolution, yet few at the time recognized that it signaled the beginning of the end of the war. Here and there, battles were still waged. Patriot guerrillas in the South continued their raids. British troops still occupied the major Southern port cities. New York still bristled with redcoats. Clinton's troops remained there, in fact, for another two years.

Not until April 1783 did George Washington officially declare the war over. Yet in London, when news of Yorktown reached Lord North, the British prime minister, he knew exactly what it meant.

"Oh God!" he groaned. "It is all over."

Camp followers fold a quilt in an officer's tent at a recent Yorktown reenactors' encampment. The stars were aligned in favor of America at Yorktown: Cornwallis attempted to evacuate his army on the night of October 16, 1781, but a terrific storm prevented their escape across the York River.

Soldiers Sculpt the Landscape into

$\mathcal{A}$ soldier in the 1700s used a shovel and ax as well as he shot a musket. Many revolutionary campaigns, from Bunker Hill to Yorktown, required a tremendous amount of digging and chopping. Soldiers built fortifications, sometimes overnight, using only the materials found at hand—primarily dirt and sticks. Whether or not a soldier ever had to attack or defend an earthwork, he was likely to have known the arduous labor of constructing one.

First, men creating a breastwork had to dig the ditch, or parallel. The earth moved out of the ditch was used to make the accompanying parapet, or wall. A ditch dug eight feet deep meant a wall built eight feet high. Soldiers made their own versions of sandbags, packing dirt into U-shaped baskets, or gabions, made from sticks, reeds, and grasses. Measuring three

Earthworks snake around the hills and fields near Yorktown. The allies broke ground for siege works on October 6, 1781, digging feverishly through a rainy night, building redoubts, and creating a trench more than a mile long.

The Revolutionary War

Trenches and Walls

to four feet high and up to three feet wide, they were laid side by side as foundations for the walls. Ten-foot-long bundles of sticks called fascines were packed tightly together, then covered with sod, to make it difficult to cross the walls: 18th-century barbed wire. Some earthworks were also protected by a series of sharpened logs, laid in a pattern angling outwards, called abatis.

Fighting soldiers rarely dismantled the breastworks they had built. Their jobs were not to stay and work afterwards but to go on to the next battle zone. After Cornwallis's capitulation, though, with no more fighting in sight, George Washington ordered all earthworks built by Americans leveled, in order to restore the landscape as usable farmland. A few revolutionary breastworks still remain. Hordes of engineering tools as well have been unearthed at Yorktown and other sites.

Once the war was over,
the Revolution continued—
not on the battlefields, but in the legislature.

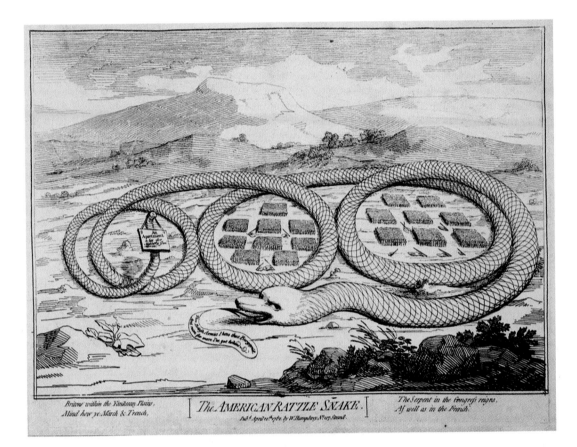

America as a rattlesnake coils around the armies of Burgoyne and Cornwallis in a
1782 etching by prominent English caricaturist James Gillray. Says the snake,
"Two British Armies I have thus Burgoyn'd And room for more I've got behind."
By this time, much of Britain was sympathetic to the American cause.

Chapter Eight

The flames of war still flickered around the country, but by the fall of 1781, they were beginning to die out. Money and energy were scarcer than ever on both sides. The events at Yorktown delivered the kind of knockout punch that in modern times might have ended hostilities, but news traveled so slowly in the 1700s, it would take a while for assessment and reaction to occur. Conflicts continued. Though the formal battles were over, fierce guerrilla struggles would bloody the southern landscape for another year, as they would the midwestern territory then known as the North-west. Meanwhile, a full-scale war between Great Britain and France was breaking out in the West Indies.

While forces had been assembling at Yorktown, the resourceful Nathanael Greene was still doggedly carrying on in the South. On September 8, 1781, his little army in South Carolina fought the Battle of Eutaw Springs—the last major action of the war, since Yorktown never developed into an all-out battle. Greene's veterans fought hard and held the British, finally driving them away, and it appeared as though they had actually won the battle.

But when the hungry soldiers found rum and food left behind in the British camp, they could not help but dive in. The British, seeing the opportunity to regain their losses, marched right back into military engagement and drove the unsuspecting patriots from the field. Once again, Greene had to chalk one up as a tactical loss. But by inflicting 800 casualties and forcing the British to pull back to Charleston, he triumphed anyway.

Right after Yorktown, Washington tried to persuade the French naval commander, de Grasse, to stay and help him remove the British presence in Charleston, but the admiral begged off. He set sail, returning to the West Indies. Washington went back north, determined

PRECEDING PAGES: George Washington rides in triumph through New York on November 25, 1783. After seven years of occupying the city, the British were gone.

to keep an ongoing vigil over the British forces still in New York. He tried to find ways to hold his army together until he could come up with a strategy that would allow them finally to recapture the city for the American side.

IT WAS NOW UP TO THE POLITICIANS TO NEGOTIATE a lasting peace. In London, the ministry that had kept the war alive was beginning to crumble. In February 1782, a motion to stop aggression against the Americans was barely defeated in Parliament. A few days later, though, a slightly revised but similar motion passed.

Charming, witty, and brilliant in diplomacy, Benjamin Franklin won over the French court at the beginning and after the end of the Revolution. He cultivated the image of a homespun American philosopher, which greatly appealed to sophisticated French public opinion.

The Revolutionary War

At first, George III tried to marshal support to continue fighting the war. But on March 20, he had to face the fact that the cause was hopeless. He accepted the resignation of Lord North, the prime minister, who had grown tired of the conflict and all that it entailed. At one point King George entertained the idea of abdicating, so much did Parliament's decision to end the war seem a rejection of his authority. He quickly dropped that dramatic posture, though, and capitulated to the new state of affairs.

The new prime minister, the Marquis of Rockingham, saw the writing on the wall: The war was over. The work cut out for him was

to clean house. Clinton wanted out, but there were still thousands of British troops in America. Someone had to be in charge. To replace Clinton, Rockingham sent Sir Guy Carleton, defender of Quebec in the winter of 1775-76. At the same time, the British made moves toward negotiating a settlement with ministers from all the countries with which they had recently engaged in conflicts: France, Spain, and, for the first time, the new United States of America.

Sent to New York, Carleton's instructions were to deploy British military force in America for defensive purposes only. At first, he naively thought he could convince the Americans to accept a peace settlement that kept them as part of the British Empire. He was quickly disabused of this notion. He found, in fact, that Americans even put up resistance when he tried to use his troops against the French.

Negotiations with foreign powers had never been an issue, as long as America was treated as a cluster of colonies and not an independent

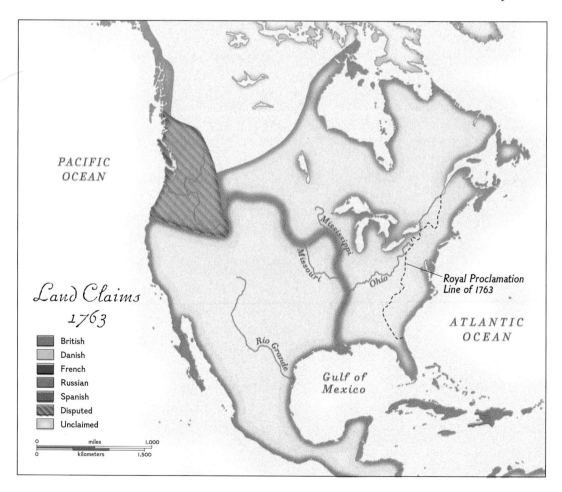

The Revolutionary War

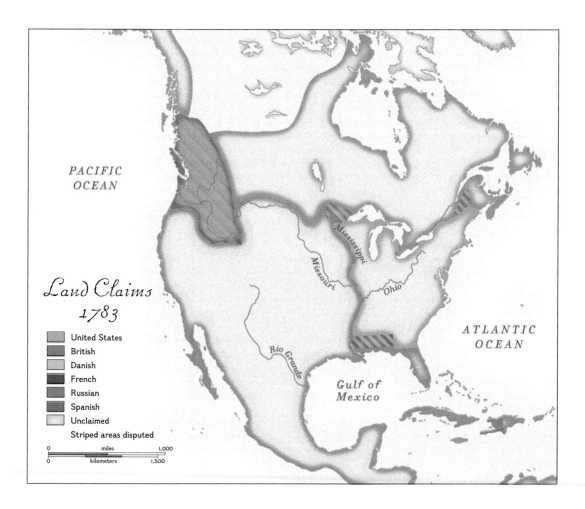

PACIFIC
OCEAN

Land Claims
1783

United States
British
Danish
French
Russian
Spanish
Unclaimed
Striped areas disputed

| miles | 1,000 |
| kilometers | 1,500 |

Mississippi

Missouri

Ohio

ATLANTIC
OCEAN

Rio Grande

Gulf of
Mexico

nation. As early as 1779, Congress had appointed statesman John Adams to negotiate with Britain, but he had not yet done so. In 1781, Congress designated four others to join him in a peace commission: Benjamin Franklin, John Jay, Thomas Jefferson, and Henry Laurens.

THERE WAS NO NEAT BEGINNING to the peace process, and diplomats, especially Franklin, were hard at work while soldiers were still on the battlefields. A meeting was planned for Paris. Jefferson, shaken by the recent death of his wife, decided not to make the trip. Laurens, who had been minister to the Netherlands, was captured on the Atlantic and held in the Tower of London for too long to be of service. That left New Yorker John Jay, minister to Spain; Adams, who had been in The Hague trying to borrow money for America; and Franklin, already in Paris. In this threesome, the venerable Franklin, age 75, became the major spokesman for his countrymen.

The talks went on through the spring and summer of 1782 before

As a new nation was carved out of North America, Europe's grip on the continent loosened. After the French and Indian Wars in 1763, Britain had the upperhand on the continent. Twenty years later, British territory amounted to Canada alone.

James Madison

The father of the Constitution, James Madison made his main contribution to the Revolution after the war was over. In 1769, at the age of 18, the trim, small-voiced, five-foot-six Virginian rode to the College of New Jersey in Princeton. He finished a four-year course of study in two years. Overwork led to bouts of epileptoid hysteria and a fear of early death. Unfit for military service, Madison studied law at home and in 1776 was elected to the Virginia convention. Four years later the state sent him to the Continental Congress. In 1787 Madison represented Virginia at the Constitutional Convention, where one delegate commented that he "always comes forward the best informed Man of any point in debate." His tireless efforts led in large part to the shaping and ratification of the U.S. Constitution between 1787 and 1789. Later, by sponsoring the first ten amendments to the Constitution, Madison created the Bill of Rights.

From 1809 to 1817, James Madison served as the fourth U.S. President, guiding the young country through another war with Britain. But his reputation rests chiefly on his being a great political theorist. "If men were angels, no government would be necessary," he observed in *The Federalist* in 1788. "If angels were to govern men, neither external nor internal controls on government would be necessary."

much progress was made. In July, when Prime Minister Rockingham died, he was replaced by the Earl of Shelburne, a brilliant politician whose idea was to offer a generous settlement as a way of cementing a profitable trade treaty between America and Britain. The problem was that if he said this out loud, he would appear to be angling to put America back into a position of colonial dependency.

The French had their own agenda, having entered the war for reasons other than to liberate the American colonies. War with Great Britain had swollen the French monarchy's debt tremendously, contributing to a growing fiscal crisis that would help foment violent regime change in another ten years. For now, though, King Louis XVI wanted to negotiate separate agreements with America and Britain, to preserve French interests in both the New World and Europe. In fact, all the principals were busy trying to play one side against another, the whole thing a complex series of deals that took many months to hammer out.

In the end, France came out the biggest loser. Beaten by the British in the Caribbean and in India, they were lucky to retain their few rich sugar islands in the West Indies and trading posts in the East. Spain, which had entered the war to retake Gibraltar from Britain, failed to secure that prize. But Spain did gain the Mediterranean island of Minorca and the British colonies of East and West Florida— today's Florida, plus the Gulf coastlands that are part of today's Alabama and Mississippi.

Benjamin Franklin had been around long enough to develop close ties to several of the French and British negotiators, and he knew he could not be outsmarted by any of them. So when British diplomats proposed a private deal that would cut out the French, shrewd old Franklin was amenable. French ministers agreed to the talks between the British and American commissioners, as long as they were included in the final treaty. By September Franklin and Jay were dealing with the British, not bothering to keep the French informed, and ignoring congressional instructions to consult with France while negotiating peace.

When the American commissioners began, they were operating on the general principle of obtaining independence first, then going on to other issues. In the end they got much more than they had hoped for. Authorized by Shelburne to interact with the commissioners of the "Thirteen United States"—for the first time, Britain officially used that term—a British negotiator met with Franklin and Jay, and talks proceeded.

A pitcher tallies the results of the nation's first census: In 1790 some four million people called the United States home. With a population of nearly 748,000, Virginia ranked first among the states; least populous was South Carolina, with less than 25,000.

By October 8, the ministers had drafted a preliminary peace agreement, to be finalized after the conclusion of a treaty between Britain and France. Among the articles of peace were the recognition of an independent United States of America, American fishing rights on the Grand Banks off Newfoundland, the end of all hostilities, the evacuation of British troops from American soil, and free navigation by both countries of the Mississippi River. Also, Congress was to "recommend" that states return property and rights to loyalists, but the language made it easy for the new country to overlook rather than to act on this provision. Finally, the boundaries for the United States were agreed upon, shaped much as Congress had hoped to see: west to the

Mississippi and north to more or less to the current borderline. Franklin and Jay tried to get Canada as the 14th state, but finally conceded it to Britain. The bargaining continued until the end of November. The United States worked out a deal to gain possession of Florida, although it was not finally resolved until a 1795 agreement with Spain, long after Britain was out of the picture in that region. The vague boundary lines between Maine and Canada were finally drawn clearly in 1842.

For all practical purposes, a workable peace had been achieved. Congress ratified the treaty in April, and all parties signed it in Paris on September 3, 1783. British critics complained that their new ministry had given away too much. North lost the war and Shelburne lost the peace, they complained. Carping afterwards was easier than negotiating, which in turn was nothing compared to actual fighting. And it is likely that a majority of English citizens did not support the war in the first place.

ON A BRISK DAY IN LATE NOVEMBER, the last of the British troops, not even a thousand strong, marched down through Manhattan Island and into the ships waiting at harbor where, seven years earlier, their legions had gathered as conquerors. Bitter in this final exit, the British cut the flagpole lines at the Battery. But within a few minutes, new lines were strung and the Stars and Stripes was hoisted. It rippled in the breeze as the old foe sailed away.

The governor of New York feted Washington and his officers in grand style, depleting his wine cellar in the process. Then, on December 4, 1783, in New York's Fraunces Tavern, the American commander bade his officers an emotional farewell. His voice caught as he spoke off the cuff.

"With a heart full of love and gratitude," he said, "I now take leave of you. I most devoutly wish that your later days may be as prosperous and happy as your former ones have been glorious and honorable." In the final tally, Washington had won but three of the nine major battles he had fought, yet through determination and devotion, he and his forces had won the war. The officers present made toasts, then one by one they stepped up to embrace their unwavering commander. No words were spoken. The tears said everything.

Washington then hurried south. He wanted to reach his beloved Virginia home, Mount Vernon, before Christmas. In every town and every village through which he traveled, he met with delay, as

well-wishers turned out to hail him. In Annapolis on December 23, he formally resigned his commission before the Continental Congress. On Christmas Eve, he crossed the Potomac into Virginia. He spurred his horse along the bank until he saw once again that bright colonnade on the river's edge. Now he could breathe a sigh of relief—he had done what he set out to do, and now he could come home.

Thomas Paine is said to have once observed that no army can conquer an idea. Likewise, in later years, John Adams wrote, "The Revolution was effected before the war commenced in the minds and hearts of the people." True enough. But Washington might have added that without warriors willing to die for what they believed, the idea would have remained just that—an idea.

DURING THE FIRST FEW YEARS AFTER THE WAR, the American Revolution continued—not on the battlefield, but in the legislature. To be sure, there was now a United States of America, but to call the states "united" was more an ideal than a legal fact. Congress in 1781 had approved a document called the Articles of Confederation, which

FOLLOWING PAGES: On the banks of the Potomac in Northern Virginia, Washington's Mount Vernon looks much as it did in the winter of 1783 on its master's return. The tree in the foreground is said to have been planted by George Washington himself.

*In framing a government which is to be administered by men over men,
the great difficulty lies in this: You must first enable the government to control the governed;
and in the next place, oblige it to control itself.*

JAMES MADISON, *The Federalist, Number 51*, FEBRUARY 6, 1788

kept central authority so weak that it was a government in little more than name only: It was simply a confederation of sovereign states. Americans had just struggled to free themselves from strong, central governance by the British Parliament, and this is the way they wanted their new nation to operate. To most Americans, strong governments ran the risk of becoming despotic. Republics were supposed to be weak, to ensure a virtuous government. From 1781 to 1787, the United States government followed this principle. Its job was to make war and peace, coin money, create a postal service, manage Indian affairs—and that was about all. Most importantly, it could not collect taxes.

Lest this sound appealing, consider the state of the union in the mid-1780s. Without enough funds, soldiers and officers could not be paid. That meant that the fledgling Navy had to be scrapped. Borders and maritime trade could not be protected. Furthermore, the sovereignty of the new United States was sketchy, or seemed to be in the eyes of the nations with whom it needed to do business. Britain did not deign to send a minister to the United States. John Adams was graciously accepted as an envoy in England, but he felt frustrated by the crown's continued sluggishness in removing British troops from all the forts in the Northwest Territory. Such a move would be considered, he was told, once America paid its debts. The troops did not leave for several more years. Likewise, Jefferson was practically ineffectual in France. Spain's minister to the United States pugnaciously let the new kid know that, treaty or no treaty, the southern Mississippi Valley was still Spanish territory.

With neither chief executive nor federal courts, the government had little authority. Instablity and economic depression finally led to mutiny in Massachusetts, when a group of farmers, threatened with losing their debt-ridden property, tried to take over a national arsenal in January 1787. Led by Daniel Shays, who had served as an officer in the Revolution, a band of 1,200 converged on the Springfield arsenal on January 26. The governor called out the state militia, who forced the rebels back. In the process, they killed four of Shays's followers.

The Revolutionary War

Things were getting unruly. It was time for Congress to act. Some of the revolutionary leaders recognized an opportunity. Isolated by oceans from Europe and the rest of the world, and surrounded by natural resources beyond reckoning, here was a unique chance to create a nation from scratch, one that could be truly worthy of the liberty for which they had fought.

From May 25 to September 17, a group of about 55 of America's best educated, most influential leaders—among them, lawyers, merchants, and planters—met in Philadelphia. They had been chosen by special conventions to represent every state except Rhode Island. They convened to discuss, argue, sweat in the heat, and compromise.

Lawless times followed the war. Depressed states tried to raise money by taxation. In 1786-87, rebels fought with government supporters during Shays's Rebellion, a series of Massachusetts uprisings over unfair taxes and economic instability.

They ultimately turned out a document considered one of the most important in the history of the world. Members of Congress had reluctantly authorized their meeting, agreeing to consider their suggested improvements to the Articles of Confederation. They were shocked to learn that this new body proposed to abandon the Articles and establish a different structure of government.

George Washington was chosen to preside over the Philadelphia Convention. Octogenarian Benjamin Franklin hovered about as a guiding spirit. Alexander Hamilton—Washington's aide-de-camp and the nation's future secretary of

Home from the war, George Washington relaxes with his wife, Martha, her grandson, George Washington Parke Custis, and her granddaughter, Eleanor Parke Custis, in this 1783 portrait. After a short time as a country squire, he returned to public office and served as President until 1797.

the treasury—sat in on a few sessions, but he so ardently believed in a powerful central government that even other strong government advocates could not take him seriously. Pennsylvanian James Wilson and New Yorker Gouverneur Morris were perhaps the most outspoken at the convention. Elbridge Gerry of Massachusetts, who also had a lot to say, later became Vice President under James Madison. From South Carolina came Charles Pinckney, future Senator, and John Rutledge, future Supreme Court Justice.

The person who became the visionary leader of this august gathering was James Madison, the soft-spoken Virginian who earned the title of "architect of the Constitution." One problem the convention had to tackle was representation in Congress. Representatives from small states wanted an equal voice, while those from large states thought population size should grant them more seats. After all, larger states would pay higher taxes. The compromise solution was a bicameral legislature with a lower house representing states in proportion to population—the House of Representatives—and an upper house with two members from each state, no matter what its size—the Senate.

But in assessing population, they questioned, how should one count the slaves? Northerners at the convention thought slaves should be counted the same as whites for purposes of taxation, but not for representation. Southerners naturally argued for the opposite, there

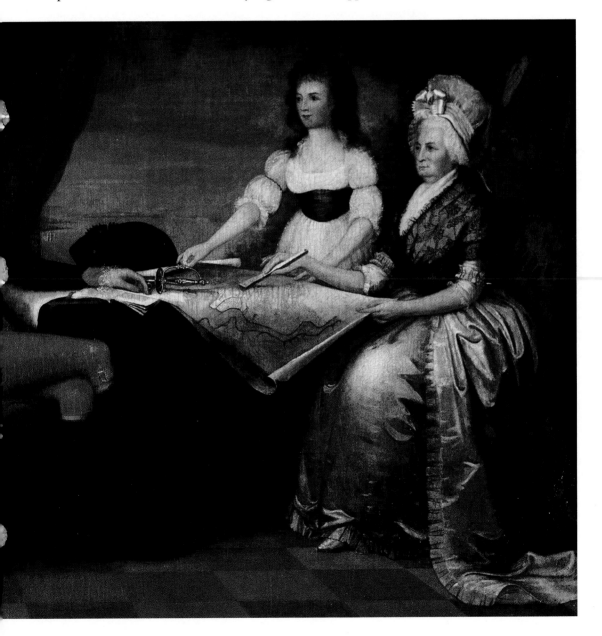

being so many more slaves in the South. Madison proposed having five slaves count as three whites for both purposes, and the motion carried. Constitutional phrasing also distinguished the legislative, executive, and judiciary branches of government, and described the checks and balances necessary to keep any one of those three branches from gaining too much power.

The framers decided to put the Constitution to a vote in every state. If conventions representing at least 9 of the 13 states approved it, it would become the law of the land. Within a year, it was adopted. Representatives in some of the holdout states—New York, Virginia, and North Carolina—worried that the Constitution lacked a Bill of Rights. It was fine to spell out the form and function of government, but what about the rights of the governed? What protected citizens from the kind of tyranny they had fought against? George Mason of Virginia felt so strongly about this, he did not sign the Constitution, one of the few representatives who did not. By 1791, a Bill of Rights was added to the U.S. Constitution.

Some assailed the Constitution for not protecting Southern interests. Patrick Henry foresaw that if it did not shield slavery, the federal government would target the practice. For these and lesser quibbles, "Light-Horse Harry" Lee, the father of Robert E. Lee, denounced Patrick Henry. "I love the people of the north," Lee said, "not because they have adopted the Consitution, but because I fought with them as my countrymen."

THE CONSTITUTION WAS NOT PERFECT. It would be sorely tested in the future. But it was flexible enough to adapt to the changing needs of a growing nation. That it remains in effect into its third century and continues to serve as a model for political change around the globe is testimony to its enduring strength.

It came as no surprise when the electoral college unanimously designated George Washington President. In the spring of 1789, he mounted his horse and headed north again, crowds cheering along the way. Seven years earlier, when a colonel had suggested to Washington that he might become king, many officers serving under him agreed. But the general dismissed the idea out of hand, saying, "If you have any regard for your country, banish these thoughts from your mind."

Washington had the greatness of character to understand that the Revolution was not his personal victory, but something much bigger. Reluctantly, he agreed to serve his country once more. Ultimately he

Under the steady gaze of the Statue of Liberty, tall ships like those that met in battle during the Revolution sail New York Harbor on July 4, 2000. An 1884 gift from France, the statue memorializes the alliance between the two nations that won the Revolutionary War.

The Revolutionary War

refused a third term as President, though, fearing that if he were to die in office, it would establish the precedent of a lifelong presidency. At the age of 65, George Washington went home and spent the final two and a half years of his life on his plantation, Mount Vernon.

The Revolution to which he and the other American heroes had pledged their sacred honor, and their lives, was over. It was now up to the American people to make something of it.

Designing a Stars and Stripes To

*N*o one knows for sure who designed the United States flag or whether it flew during any Revolutionary War battle. General Washington was issued no official American flags to fly until the spring of 1783, when peace was being negotiated.

Various heraldic standards began to appear in the early years of the Revolution. One popular motif was the rattlesnake—a native American reptile much feared by European soldiers—on a yellow or red-and-white striped field, often accompanied by the phrase, "Don't Tread on Me." From 1775 to 1777 the unofficial American flag was the Continental Colors, or Grand Union flag. Consisting of 13 alternating red and white stripes with a British Union Jack in the upper lefthand corner, the Grand Union suited colonies still attached to the mother country.

After the Declaration of Independence, the main business of the day was to fight a war. But Congress found time on June 14, 1777, to issue a resolution "that the flag of the United States be

Be an Emblem Forever

thirteen stripes, alternate red and white; that the union be thirteen stars, white in a blue field, representing a new constellation." Flags began appearing with different arrangements—13 stars in a circle, or 12 circling a central star, or (the most popular) stars in horizontal rows. Historians have been unable to verify whether Betsy Ross designed this flag, and no one is certain who first called it the Stars and Stripes. Betsy Ross did make flags for Pennsylvania, but the first we know of her association with the Stars and Stripes is when her grandson claimed in 1870 that she designed it at the request of George Washington. It is likely that Francis Hopkinson, artist and delegate to the Continental Congress, had some say in the design.

The new American flag was first saluted in a foreign port on February 14, 1778, when John Paul Jones sailed the *Ranger* into Quiberon Bay, France. A flag at the battle of Yorktown in 1781 inspired Pvt. Joseph Martin to write, "I felt a secret pride swell in my heart when I saw the 'star-spangled banner' waving majestically."

When Vermont and Kentucky entered the Union in 1795, two new stars and two new stripes were added. By 1818, though, it became clear that as states increased, the flag would be cluttered with stripes. Congress mandated a return to just 13, to represent the original colonies, plus a star for every state. No one put in writing why red, white, and blue were the chosen colors for the flag, but Congress approved them for the Great Seal of the United States, interpreting red to stand for courage, white for purity, and blue for justice.

This flag, opposite, reportedly flew at a Pennsylvania public reading of the Declaration of Independence on July 8, 1776. Below, the Stars and Stripes rose over New York Harbor when the British departed in November 1783.

About the Author

John Thompson is the author of six National Geographic books, including *America's Historic Trails* and the forthcoming *Wildlands of the Upper South*. He has written numerous articles on travel and natural history and is currently researching a book on Benedict Arnold's march to Quebec. His travels have taken him all over the country for assignments that have included every state except Wisconsin and Texas. He lives with his family in Charlottesville, Virginia.

Touring the American Revolution

Scores of Revolutionary War battlefields and other sites have been preserved or memorialized. Visits to some of the key sites will help bring the Revolution into sharper focus.

The Boston area is filled with landmarks of momentous Revolutionary-era events. The popular 2.5-mile **Freedom Trail** begins in Boston Common and ends across the Charles River at the **Bunker Hill Monument**, scene of the 1775 battle. The Freedom Trail passes by the 1729 **Old South Meeting House**, where Samuel Adams addressed crowds; the **Old State House**, where the Boston Massacre occurred; the 1742 **Faneuil Hall** and its museum; the modest clapboard **Paul Revere House**; and the **Old North Church**, where lanterns warned of the British approach. The first shots of the war were fired in **Lexington** (20 miles northwest of Boston) and **Concord** (5 miles west of Lexington), which include several sites and buildings of historic interest.

In northern New York, visitors can explore **Fort Ticonderoga**, near the southern end of Lake Champlain, captured by British Gen. John Burgoyne in 1777. Burgoyne himself was defeated by Gen. Horatio Gates at Bemis Heights, now commemorated at the **Saratoga National Historical Park**, a 3,200-acre battlefield with a visitor center and scenic drive. Burgoyne surrendered to Gates a few miles north, at the town now known as Schuylerville, where there is an imposing monument. The U.S. Military Academy at West Point, established in 1802, was the site of major fortifications, and the **West Point Museum** contains many artifacts pertaining to the Revolutionary War.

In New Jersey, the **Monmouth Battlefield State Park** commemorates the major clash in June 1778 between the forces of Generals Washington and Clinton. To the north, displays at the **Morristown National Historical Park** detail the hard life of the Continental Army, particularly during the cruel winter of 1779-1780. On the Delaware River in Bucks County, Pennsylvania, the **Washington Crossing Historic Park** helps evoke the dramatic story of Washington's daring river advance in December 1776, a pivotal event in the war.

Philadelphia boasts numerous Revolutionary-era buildings, concentrated for the most part in a 12-block zone designated **Independence National Historical Park**. Included are **Franklin Court**, home of Benjamin Franklin, and **Independence Hall**, a UNESCO World Heritage Site where the Declaration of Independence was adopted and the Constitution was drafted. About 20 miles northwest of the city, **Valley Forge National Historical Park** preserves the 1777-78 winter campsite of the Continental Army. Vincennes, Indiana, site of a significant battle in the fight for the Old Northwest, now is home to the **George Rogers Clark National Historical Park.**

In Charleston, South Carolina, **Fort Moultrie**, part of Fort Sumter National Monument, withstood a furious British bombardment in 1776. In northwestern South Carolina, **King's Mountain National Military Park** celebrates the turning-point victory of 1780. In January 1781, American forces followed up with another success nearby at **Cowpens National Battlefield**, also open to the public.

Visitors can imagine how the armies swirled into North Carolina and met at the area now commemorated as the **Guilford Courthouse National Military Park**. Here, in March 1781, Nathanael Greene lost the field but inflicted great casualties on the British. The war's showdown came in October 1781 at Yorktown, Virginia. The sequence of momentous events is displayed at the **Yorktown Battlefield**, part of the Colonial National Historical Park.

For locations important after the end of military action, one can travel to **Washington's Headquarters** on the Hudson River at Newburgh, New York, where the general resided from April 1782 to August 1783. In New York City, visitors can visit a museum and dine 18th-century-style at **Fraunces Tavern**, where in December 1783 Washington took moving leave of his officers after the last British troops left the newly independent United States.

Further Reading

John R. Alden, *A History of the American Revolution* (Knopf, 1969)

Bernard Bailyn, *Faces of the Revolution: Personalities and Themes in the Struggle for American Independence* (Knopf, 1990)

Mark M. Boatner III, *Encyclopedia of the American Revolution* (David McKay, 1966)

Henry Steele Commager and Richard B. Morris, eds., *The Spirit of Seventy-Six: The Story of the American Revolution as Told by Participants* (Castle, 2002)

Howard Fast, *The Crossing* (William Morrow, 1971)

Thomas Fleming, *Liberty! The American Revolution* (Viking, 1997)

Richard M. Ketchum, *Saratoga: Turning Point of America's Revolutionary War* (Henry Holt, 1997)

Robert Leckie, *George Washington's War: The Saga of the American Revolution* (HarperCollins, 1992)

Robert Middlekauff, *The Glorious Cause: The American Revolution, 1763-1789* (Oxford Univ. Press, 1982)

Kenneth Roberts, ed., *March to Quebec: Journals of the Members of Arnold's Expedition* (Doubleday, 1938)

James L. Stokesbury, *A Short History of the American Revolution* (William Morrow, 1991)

Gordon S. Wood, *The Radicalism of the American Revolution* (Vintage Books, 1991)

Index

Boldface indicates illustrations

Illustration Credits

LC = Library of Congress

1, John Muller, from *Treatise of Artillery*, 1768; 2-3, John C. McRae after a painting by F.A. Charman, LC; 6-7, The Granger Collection, NY; 8, Burstein Collection/CORBIS; 10, LC; 11, Jeremiah Meyer, Courtesy of the National Portrait Gallery, London; 12-13, Bob Krist; 14, LC; 15, Colonial Williamsburg Foundation; 17, Sir William Beechey, Courtesy of the National Portrait Gallery, London; 18-19, Bettmann/CORBIS; 20, The Daughters of the American Revolution Museum, Washington, D.C. On loan from Boston Tea Party Chapter; 21 & 23, Joel Sartore; 24 **(both)**, Hulton|Archive by Getty Images; 25, Mary Evans Picture Library; 26-27, W.B. Wollen, with permission of the National Army Museum, London; 28, Joel Sartore; 30, Courtesy American Antiquarian Society; 31, Joel Sartore; 35, Hulton|Archive by Getty Images; 36 **(both)**, Courtesy of Massachusetts Historical Society; 37, LC; 38-39, Winthrop Chandler, *The Battle of Bunker Hill*, Courtesy Museum of Fine Arts, Boston: Gift of Mr. & Mrs. Gardner Richardson. Reproduced with permission. © 2003 Museum of Fine Arts, Boston. All Rights Reserved; 42-43, Lee Snider/CORBIS; 45, Bob Krist; 46, Attributed to John Durand, The Connecticut Historical Society, Hartford, Connecticut; 47, LC; 48-49, John Trumbull, Yale University Art Gallery; 50, Leif Skoogfors/CORBIS; 52 & 53, LC; 54-55, José Fuste Raga/CORBIS; 56, Collection of The New-York Historical Society, Neg. #1925.6; 59, LC; 60-61, James Smillie from *Battles of the United States By Sea and Land*, 1858; 64-65, Dominique Serres, Courtesy U. S. Naval Academy Museum; 66-67, Howard Pyle, Wilmington Society of the Fine Arts, Delaware Art Center; 68, Historical Society of Pennsylvania; 69, Sam Abell; 70, Maryland Historical Society; 71, LC; 72-73, John Trumbull, Yale University Art Gallery; 74, Bob Krist; 78-79, Michael S. Yamashita/CORBIS; 80, William Mercer, Atwater Kent Museum of Philadelphia; 82, Courtesy of The National Portrait Gallery, London; 84-85, Ping Amranand; 86, Courtesy National Park Service, Museum Management Program and Guilford Courthouse National Military Park. Bullet Mold GUCO 1506. www.cr.nps.gov/museum/exhibits/revwar; 87, New York State Historical Association, Cooperstown; 89, LC; 90-91, Howard Smith, courtesy CNA Insurance; 93, David Muench/CORBIS; 95, Bob Krist; 96-97, William B.T. Trego, Courtesy National Center for the American Revolution; 98, The Granger Collection, NY; 100, Ted Spiegel; 102-103, John Lewis Stage; 104, Robert Llewellyn; 107, Hulton|Archive by Getty Images; 108-109, Emanuel Leutze, 1854, Collection of the University Art Museum of the University of California, Berkeley. Gift of Mrs. Mark Hopkins; 110, George F. Mobley; 111, Bettmann/CORBIS; 112-113, Christie's Images/ CORBIS; 117, Galen Rowell/CORBIS; 118, Collection of The New-York Historical Society, Neg. #48257; 119, Charles Willson Peale, Courtesy of The Mount Vernon Ladies' Association; 120-121, Sir Richard Paton, Courtesy U.S. Naval Academy Museum; 122, Stephen G. St. John/NGS Image Collection; 124-125, Hulton|Archive by Getty Images; 126-127, James Randklev/Larry Ulrich Stock; 128, Courtesy Hargrett Rare Book & Manuscript Library/ University of Georgia Libraries; 129, Ferdinand de Brackeleer, Courtesy Hugh S. Watson, Jr.; 130-131, Geoffrey Clements/CORBIS; 133, Thomas Gainsborough, Courtesy of The National Portrait Gallery, London; 134-135, From *Battles of the United States By Sea and Land*, 1858; 136, Hulton|Archive by Getty Images; 138-139, Howard Pyle, Wilmington Society of the Fine Arts, Delaware Art Center; 141, Tom Blagden/Larry Ulrich Stock; 142-143, William L. Clements Library, University of Michigan; 143, LC; 144-145, John Trumbull, Yale University Art Gallery; 146, David Muench/CORBIS; 148-149, *Battle of Kings Mountain* by Andy Thomas; 150-151, Arthur & Holly Magill Estate, Courtesy of Cowpens National Battlefield; 153, LC; 154-155, V. Zveg, Hampton Roads Naval Museum; 157, Bob Krist; 159, John B. Martin, Valentine Richmond History Center; 160-161, LC; 163, Bob Krist; 164-165, Louis-Nicolas van Blarenberghe, Private collection; 166-167, E.P. & L. Restein, LC; 168, LC; 170-171, W.O. Geller, Courtesy The Old Print Shop, NY; 174, Charles Willson Peale, LC; 177, National Museum of American History, Smithsonian Institution, Acc. #1978.0806; 177, Gail Mooney/CORBIS; 178-179, Ted Spiegel/CORBIS; 181, Bettmann/CORBIS; 182-183, Edward Savage, Andrew W. Mellon Collection, Photo © Board of Trustees, National Gallery of Art, Washington, D.C.; 185, AFP/Henny Ray Abrams/CORBIS; 186, Steve Winter, courtesy Easton Area Public Library; 187, The Granger Collection, NY.

The Revolutionary War

JOHN M. THOMPSON

Published by the National Geographic Society

John M. Fahey, Jr. President and Chief Executive Officer
Gilbert M. Grosvenor Chairman of the Board
Nina D. Hoffman Executive Vice President

Prepared by the Book Division

Kevin Mulroy Vice President and Editor-in-Chief
Charles Kogod Illustrations Director
Marianne R. Koszorus Design Director
Barbara Brownell Grogan Executive Editor

Staff for this Book

Susan Tyler Hitchcock Project and Text Editor
Peggy Archambault Art Director
Jane Menyawi Illustrations Editor
Carl Mehler Director of Maps
James Miller Researcher
Meredith Wilcox Illustrations Specialist
Matt Chwastyk,
Gregory Ugiansky,
and XNR Productions Map Research and Production
Gary Colbert Production Director
Lewis R. Bassford Production Project Manager
Robert Swanson Indexer

Manufacturing and Quality Control

Christopher A. Liedel Chief Financial Officer
Phillip L. Schlosser Managing Director
John T. Dunn Technical Director
Alan Kerr Manager

One of the world's largest nonprofit scientific and educational organizations, the NATIONAL GEOGRAPHIC SOCIETY was founded in 1888 "for the increase and diffusion of geographic knowledge." Fulfilling this mission, the Society educates and inspires millions every day through its magazines, books, television programs, videos, maps and atlases, research grants, the National Geographic Bee, teacher workshops, and innovative classroom materials. The Society is supported through membership dues, charitable gifts, and income from the sale of its educational products. This support is vital to National Geographic's mission to increase global understanding and promote conservation of our planet through exploration, research, and education.

For more information, please call 1-800-NGS LINE (647-5463) or write to the following address:

National Geographic Society
1145 17th Street N.W.
Washington, D.C. 20036-4688
U.S.A.

Visit the Society's Web site at www.nationalgeographic.com.

Composition for this book by the National Geographic Book Division.
Printed and bound by R. R. Donnelly & Sons, Willard, Ohio.
Color separations by Quad Imaging, Alexandria, Virginia.
Dust jacket printed by the Miken Co., Cheektowaga, New York.

Library of Congress Cataloging-in-Publication Data

Thompson, John M. (John Milliken), 1959-
  The Revolutionary War / by John Thompson.
    p. cm.
  Includes index.

  1. United States--History--Revolution, 1775-1783. I. Title.

E208.T47 2004
973--dc22

2003067191